THE Woodsmith COLLECTION™

BOOKCASES & SHELVES

From the Editors and Staff of
Woodsmith® Magazine

AUGUST HOME PUBLISHING COMPANY
DES MOINES, IOWA

AUGUST HOME
PUBLISHING COMPANY

Publisher   Donald B. Peschke

August Home Books

Executive Editor	Douglas L. Hicks
Art Director	Linda F. Vermie
Senior Graphic Designer	Chris Glowacki
Graphic Design Intern	Dana Ludden
Copy Editor	David Stone
Contributing Book Designer	Ted Kralicek

Contributing Staff

Editor, *Woodsmith*	Terry J. Strohman
Art Director, *Woodsmith*	Todd Lambirth
Editor, *ShopNotes*	Tim Robertson
Art Director, *ShopNotes*	Cary Christensen
Editor, *Workbench*	Chris Inman
Art Director, *Workbench*	Robert Foss
Creative Director	Ted Kralicek
Project Design Developer	Ken Munkel
Project Designers	Kent Welsh
	Ted Wong
Project Builders	Steve Curtis
	Steve Johnson
Editors	Vincent S. Ancona
	Jon Garbison
	Bryan Nelson
	Phil Totten
Illustrators	Mark Higdon
	David Kreyling
	Erich Lage
	Roger Reiland
	Kurt Schultz
	Cinda Shambaugh
	Dirk Ver Steeg
Photographers	Lark Gilmer
	Crayola England
V.P. Planning & Finance	Jon Macarthy
Production Director	George Chmielarz
Electronic Publishing	Douglas M. Lidster
Electro. Commun. Coord.	Gordon C. Gaippe

If you have any questions or comments about this book or would like subscription information about *Woodsmith*, *ShopNotes*, or *Workbench* magazines, please write to:

August Home Publishing Co.
2200 Grand Ave.
Des Moines, IA 50312

Or call: 1 800–444–7527
www.augusthome.com

INTRODUCTION

Through the years I've built quite a few bookcases and shelves in my shop. The finished project is always important; but just as important to me is the *how* and *why* of building it. Figuring out how to cut a dovetail joint on my band saw or why a shelf sags (and how to prevent it)— that's the stuff that intrigues me.

So in this book you'll find hundreds of step-by-step illustrations and detail drawings that help you understand what's *really* going on. You'll also find the plans for some jigs that will help you safely and accurately build the projects in your own shop.

In addition there are helpful tip sections (look for the boxes with dovetails). And don't miss the discussion on how to keep shelves from sagging (pages 93 to 94) and sources of supplies (page 95).

Overall, I think you'll find lots of useful information in this book — even if you don't build every project shown.

One more thing. There's a slogan I've posted in my shop and I thought you might find it useful as you work on these bookcases and shelves:

"Success is in the Details"

Give it a try,

Doug

NOTE: This is a special "Heavy-Duty Shop Edition" of *Bookcases and Shelves*. We've printed it with the following features to make it easier to use in your shop:
• UNIQUE "LAY-FLAT" BINDING — Don't be afraid to press down hard at the center between the pages. Open it anywhere and try it. It will stay flat and won't flap shut. You can't "crack" the binding.
• COLD RESISTANT — The special cold-set glue used in the binding stays strong and flexible. Even in a below-freezing garage shop.
• LAMINATED COVER — Resists dirt, liquids, stains, and many finishes.
• NON-GLARE PAPER — Easy-to-read, even under bright shop lights.

CONTENTS

Page 4

Page 16

Page 40

Page 68

SLATTED SHELF

Here's a great place to hang your hat and coat or use as a clothes rack in the kids' room. And it breaks down easily for moving or storage.

Four main parts make up this project: a shelf assembly, two end brackets with curves, and a back with "Shaker-style" birch pegs. To match the pegs, I built the project from birch.

SHELF ASSEMBLY

The shelf is made up of five slats (A) held together by three cleats (B).

SLATS. To make the slats (A), first rip five pieces of $^3/_4$"-thick stock to a common width of $1^3/_4$". Since I wanted to be able to hang the shelf on wall studs that were located 16" on center, I did a little figuring and cut the slats to 38" long.

After cutting the slats to length, round over the top edges of each slat with a $^1/_4$" roundover bit; refer to Fig. 3 on page 6.

MARK POSITION OF HOLES. Once the edges are routed, three screwholes are drilled in each slat to attach the cleats. To mark the location of these screwholes,

line up the ends of all five slats and draw lines across them with a square. Draw a line $1^3/_4$" from each end (this will position the brackets 32" on center), and at the exact center of the length; see Fig. 3.

CROSSLINES. Next, draw crosslines centered on the width of each slat. The easiest way to locate the center is with a combination square; see Fig. 1.

Set the square for just a smidgen less than half the width of a slat ($^7/_8$"), measure in from each edge, and put marks. Splitting the difference between the marks will locate the exact center. Then punch the centers with an awl.

DRILL HOLES. The screws at each of the points are sunk below the surface of the slat and covered with wood plugs; see Fig. 3. To drill the plug and screw holes, first counterbore a $^1/_2$"-dia. hole at each intersecting point. Then a $^3/_{16}$" hole is drilled the rest of the way through the slat to accept the shank of a screw.

CLEATS. With the slats complete, work can begin on the cleats (B). Since the cleats are all the same length and one end is rounded over on all of them, I found it easiest to lay out all three cleats on a single 5" wide board; see Fig. 2. Cut the board to a finished length of $9^1/_4$", and then round over one edge on one end with a $^1/_4$" roundover bit.

MARK PILOT HOLES. Before cutting the cleats apart, mark the location of the pilot hole lines for the screws; see Fig. 2. First draw a line $^3/_8$" back from the front edge. Then draw four more lines 2" apart.

Now, the three cleats can be ripped $1^1/_2$" wide. To locate the pilot holes, draw crosslines centered on the width of each cleat using the same method that was used with the slats. Finally, center punch and drill a $^3/_{32}$" hole at each point.

ASSEMBLY. With the holes drilled in both the slats and cleats, assembly can begin. Start by screwing and gluing the

EXPLODED VIEW

OVERALL DIMENSIONS:
38W x 9¾D x 10¾H

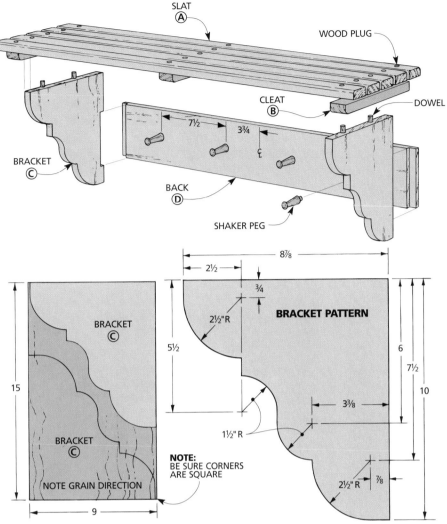

SLAT Ⓐ

WOOD PLUG

CLEAT Ⓑ

DOWEL

7½   3¾   3"

BRACKET Ⓒ

BACK Ⓓ

SHAKER PEG

MATERIALS LIST

WOOD

A	Slats (5)	¾ x 1¾ - 38
B	Cleats (3)	¾ x 1½ - 9¼
C	Brackets (2)	¾ x 8⅞ - 10
D	Back (1)	¾ x 5 - 32¾

HARDWARE SUPPLIES

(15) ½"-dia. Wood plugs
(15) No. 8 x 1" Fh woodscrews
(4) No. 8 x 1¼" Fh woodscrews
(1) ⅜"-dia. x 4"-long Dowel rod
(4) ⅞"-dia. x 3⅜"-long Birch Shaker pegs
(2) 9/16" x 1 11/16" Keyhole hangers w/screws

CUTTING DIAGRAM

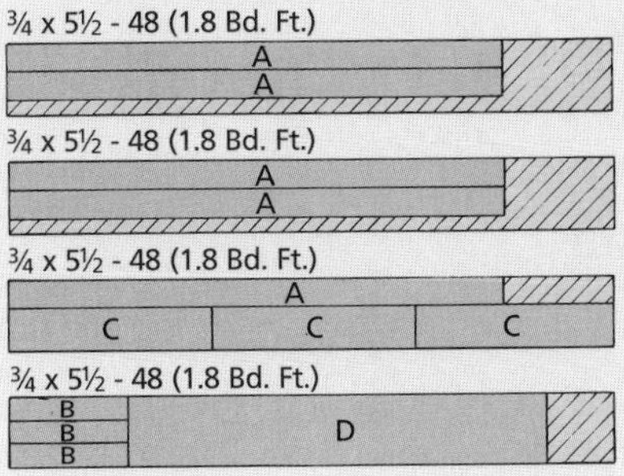

¾ x 5½ - 48 (1.8 Bd. Ft.)
| A |
| A |

¾ x 5½ - 48 (1.8 Bd. Ft.)
| A |
| A |

¾ x 5½ - 48 (1.8 Bd. Ft.)
| A | | |
| C | C | C |

¾ x 5½ - 48 (1.8 Bd. Ft.)
B	
B	D
B	

BRACKET Ⓒ

BRACKET Ⓒ

NOTE GRAIN DIRECTION

15

9

BRACKET PATTERN

8⅞
2½
¾
2½"R
5½
1½"R
3⅜
2½"R   ⅞
6
7½
10

NOTE: BE SURE CORNERS ARE SQUARE

---

two outside cleats to the first and last slats; see Fig. 3. Make sure this partial assembly is square. Then screw and glue the remaining slats and cleats together.

The final step on the shelf assembly is to glue plugs into the counterbores. Then chisel or cut them off and sand flush.

BRACKETS

The completed shelf assembly rests on two brackets (C). Both brackets are cut out of a single 9" x 15" blank made from glued-up stock; see drawing above.

After the blank is squared up, lay out a cardboard template; see the Bracket Pattern above. Then use the template to trace the brackets on the blank. Now cut, file, and sand them smooth.

MORTISE FOR KEYHOLE HANGER. The shelves are held on the wall with two nifty little metal keyhole hangers. (They're available from many woodworking mail order catalogs; see page 95.) To hold a hanger in each bracket, a 3/16"-deep, 9/16"-wide mortise is routed on the back edge; see Fig. 4. Rout the mortise by making two passes with a ½" straight bit on a router table or with a hand-held router and edge guide.

After the mortise is routed, a section of the slot needs to be drilled out to accept the head of the screw that will be in the wall; see Fig. 5.

Finally, drill holes and screw the keyhole hanger into the mortise; see Fig. 6.

STOPPED RABBET. Next, a stopped rabbet is routed on the inside back edge of each bracket to accept the back (D); see Fig. 7.

Since the stopped rabbet is to be ⅜" wide and ⅝" deep, a ⅜" rabbeting bit can be used to cut it; see Fig. 7. Start and stop the cut just a bit short of the end lines and clean it up with a sharp chisel.

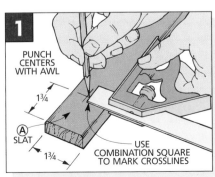

1

PUNCH CENTERS WITH AWL

1¾

Ⓐ SLAT

1¾

USE COMBINATION SQUARE TO MARK CROSSLINES

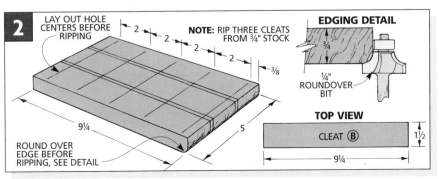

2

LAY OUT HOLE CENTERS BEFORE RIPPING

2   2   2   2   ⅜

NOTE: RIP THREE CLEATS FROM ¾" STOCK

9¼

5

ROUND OVER EDGE BEFORE RIPPING, SEE DETAIL

EDGING DETAIL

¾

¼" ROUNDOVER BIT

TOP VIEW

CLEAT Ⓑ

9¼   1½

MOUNTING THE BRACKETS. After the rabbets are routed, the brackets are mounted under the shelf assembly. I decided not to fasten the brackets permanently since I wanted to be able to take the unit apart for moving or storage. Rather, I used two short pins (dowels) in the top of each bracket to locate and stabilize the assembly; see Fig. 8.

To mount the pins, drill two holes in the bottom of the second and fourth slats. The holes are centered on the widths of these slats and located $^3/_8$" from the inside edge of the two cleats; see Fig. 8.

USING DOWEL CENTERS. After drilling the holes in the slats, use $^3/_8$" dowel centers to mark the location of the matching holes on the top edge of the brackets. Then drill these holes.

Finally, glue two short dowels into the top of each bracket to act as locating pins. Then round over the end of each dowel with sandpaper to help them slide into the matching holes.

BACK

The final piece to cut is the back (D). It's ripped to a width of 5" (to match the stopped rabbet on the bracket).

To determine the length of the back, turn the shelf assembly upside down and hold the brackets straight up against the cleats. Then measure the distance between the brackets and add the depth of both rabbets (in my case, $32^3/_4$").

After the back is cut to final length, rabbet the ends to produce $^3/_8$"-thick tongues that fit in the stopped rabbets in the brackets; see Fig. 9. Then round over the front edges with a $^1/_4$" roundover bit.

SHAKER PEGS. Now locate and drill $^1/_2$" holes, $^3/_8$" deep as shown in the Exploded View on page 5. And then glue in the Shaker Pegs.

ATTACHING THE BACK. Finally, the back is placed in the stopped rabbets in the brackets and holes are drilled for flathead woodscrews; see Fig. 10.

FINISH. To finish the shelf, I sanded all the surfaces smooth and then applied two coats of General Finishes Royal Finish (a tung oil/urethane mixture). ∎

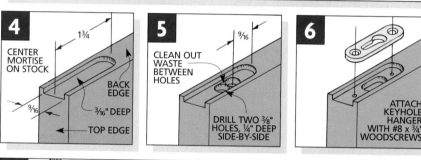

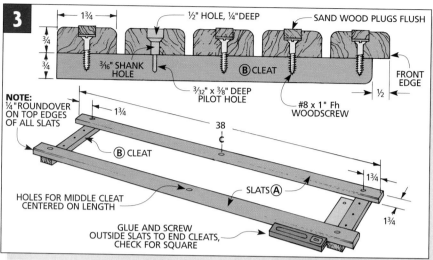

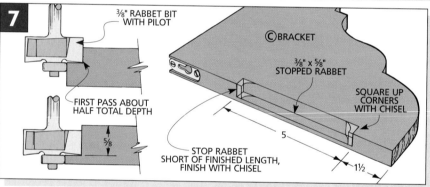

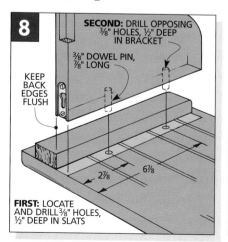

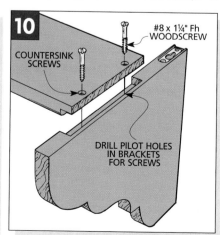

QUILT RACK

This rack has a unique feature — a spring-loaded hanging rod that makes it easy to remove and replace a folded quilt.

A lot of the quilts I've seen are hung just for display. But sometimes a quilt actually gets *used*. And that was one of the main challenges I faced when I sat down to design this quilt rack.

On some quilt racks the rod for holding the quilt is permanently attached. But for convenience, I wanted the quilt-holding rod on this rack to be removable. (Almost like the toilet paper holder in a restroom.)

By installing a spring in the end of the rod, it can be slid toward one end then pulled out for hanging up a quilt;

see inset photo above. So a person doesn't have to struggle to thread the quilt between the top of the rod and the bottom of the shelf.

Instead, the quilt can be folded exactly where you want it, then the rod slid through the fold. This way, the quilt stays folded when the rod is placed back in the rack.

WOOD. This quilt rack is made entirely out of red oak. Why not use some other kind of wood? The answer, again, has to do the with dowel rod. To keep the rod in scale with the rest of the rack, the rod is 1¹/₄" in diameter. But dowel

rod that large isn't easy to find in many types of wood. However, it is readily available in red oak from many retail woodworking stores and mail order catalogs. So I built the entire project from oak. The galley spindles can also be purchased in red oak or they can be turned on a lathe.

FINISH. In order to give the quilt rack more of an aged appearance, I stained the wood with a coat of Minwax Golden Oak.

Then, to protect the wood, I applied two coats of an oil/urethane mixture (General Finishes' Royal Finish).

EXPLODED VIEW... QUILT RACK

OVERALL DIMENSIONS:
50¾L x 10D x 10⅝H

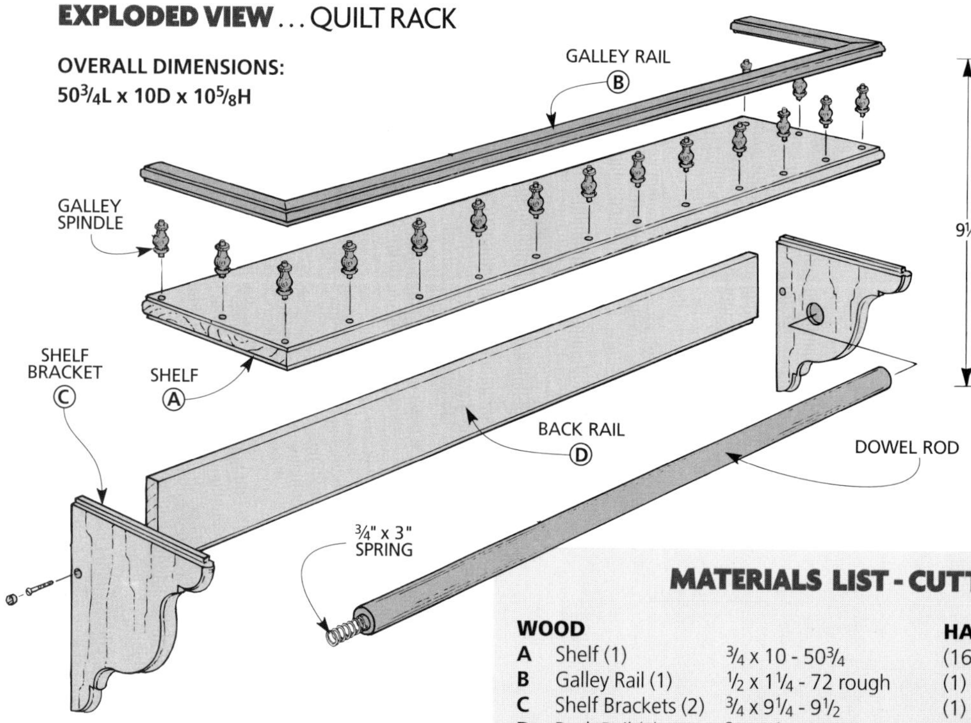

GALLEY RAIL
B
GALLEY SPINDLE
SHELF BRACKET
C
SHELF
A
BACK RAIL
D
DOWEL ROD
¾" x 3" SPRING

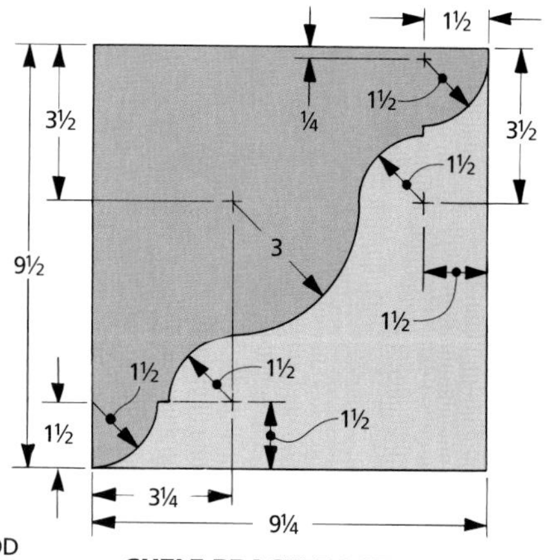

1½
3½
¼
1½
3½
1½
9½
3
1½
1½
1½
1½
1½
3¼
9¼

SHELF BRACKET PATTERN

MATERIALS LIST - CUTTING DIAGRAM

WOOD

A	Shelf (1)	¾ x 10 - 50¾
B	Galley Rail (1)	½ x 1¼ - 72 rough
C	Shelf Brackets (2)	¾ x 9¼ - 9½
D	Back Rail (1)	¾ x 3½ - 47¼

HARDWARE SUPPLIES

(16) 9/16"-dia. x 1½"-tall Galley spindles
(1) 1¼"-dia. x 47¾"-long Dowel rod
(1) ¾"-dia. x 3"-long Compression spring
(2) No. 6 x 1¼" Fh woodscrews and plugs
(2) Hanger plates with mounting screws

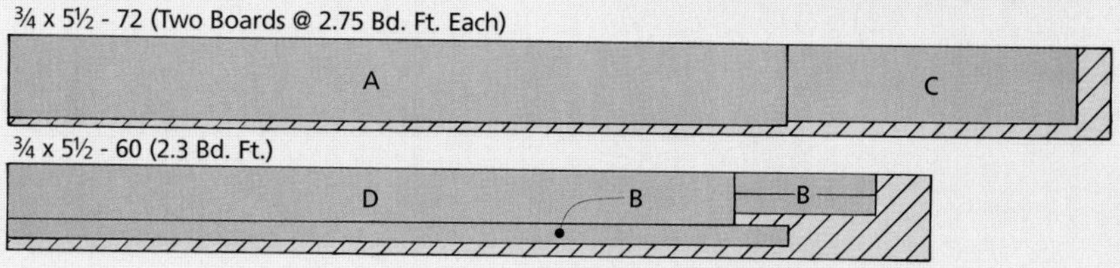

¾ x 5½ - 72 (Two Boards @ 2.75 Bd. Ft. Each)
A
C
¾ x 5½ - 60 (2.3 Bd. Ft.)
D
B
B

SHELF

I started building the quilt rack by first making the shelf. It's a long board that connects the sides (brackets) and serves as a "roof" for the quilt.

Cut to Size. First, edge glue two pieces of ¾" stock for the shelf blank; see Fig. 1. (It's hard to find flat pieces of stock that are 10" wide.) Then cut the shelf (A) to finished size.

Groove & Dadoes. Next, to create a trough for displaying plates, I routed a stopped groove along the top of the shelf near the back edge; see Fig. 1a. To do this I used a hand-held router and clamped stop blocks to the workpiece.

After routing the groove on top of the shelf, the next step is to rout stopped dadoes on the *bottom* for joining the shelf to the brackets; see Fig. 2.

Shop Note: Here, I used the router table with a stop block. On the router table, I usually move the workpiece from right to left. So depending on which end of the workpiece you're routing, it may be necessary to plunge the workpiece into the bit and then rout.

Edge Profile. Finally, I routed a decorative edge around the front and sides of the shelf; see Fig. 3. Note: By raising the roundover bit slightly above the table, a ⅛" shoulder is created as an accent; see Fig. 3a.

1

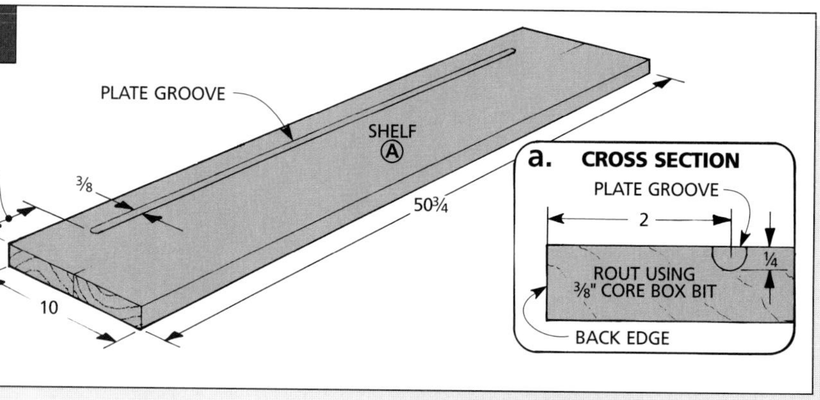

PLATE GROOVE
SHELF
A
4
⅜
50¾
10
a. CROSS SECTION
PLATE GROOVE
2
¼
ROUT USING ⅜" CORE BOX BIT
BACK EDGE

2

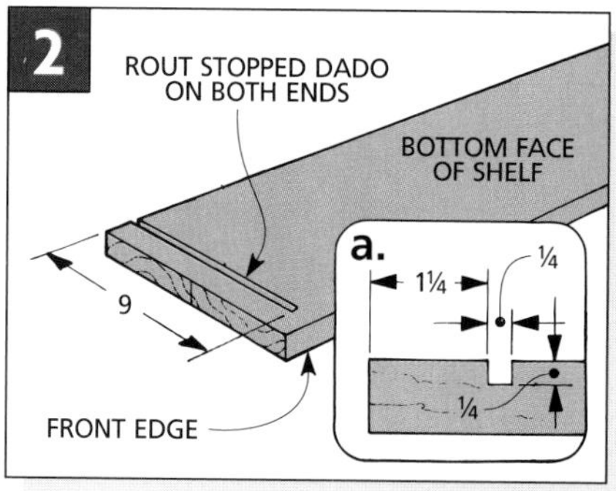

ROUT STOPPED DADO ON BOTH ENDS
BOTTOM FACE OF SHELF
9
a.
1¼
¼
¼
FRONT EDGE

3

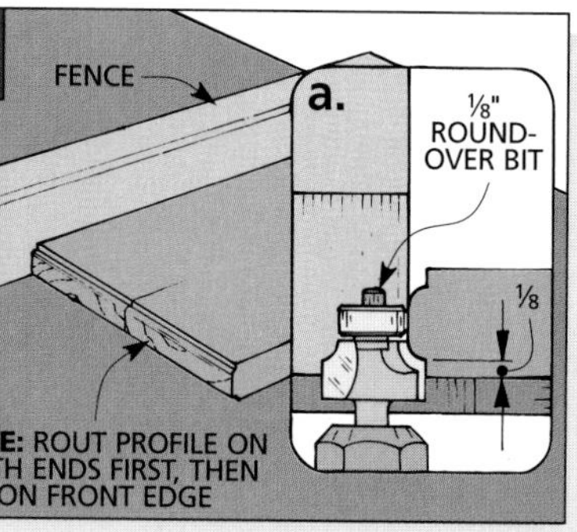

FENCE
a.
⅛" ROUND-OVER BIT
⅛
NOTE: ROUT PROFILE ON BOTH ENDS FIRST, THEN ON FRONT EDGE

GALLEY RAIL

After completing the shelf, I started work on the galley rail. This is a U-shaped "fence" that extends around the top of the shelf.

The galley rail is connected to the shelf with a series of sixteen small galley spindles.

CUT TO SIZE. The first thing to do to make the galley rail (B) is to cut three pieces to finished width for the front and side sections of the rail; see Figs. 4 and 4a.

Design Note: I resawed stock for the galley rail to $\frac{1}{2}$" thick so it wouldn't look too thick in relation to the rest of the project.

EDGE PROFILE. With the three pieces of galley rail ripped to finished width, I used my router table and a $\frac{1}{8}$" roundover bit to rout a decorative profile on all four edges of each piece; see Fig. 4a. Note: These shoulders are only $\frac{1}{16}$", not $\frac{1}{8}$" like on the shelf.

CUT MITERS. Now the three rail pieces can be mitered to fit around the top of the shelf. The front piece is mitered to the same length as the shelf, and the side pieces to the same width as the shelf; see Fig. 4. But they're not glued together at the corners yet. (It's a little easier to drill holes for the galley spindles before they're assembled.)

SPINDLE HOLES. Next, I marked the position of the holes for the spindles on the top side of the shelf; see Fig. 4. Then I used a try square to transfer the marks over onto the bottom side of the rail pieces; see Fig. 5.

Now, the shallow holes can be drilled in the top of the shelf; see Fig. 6.

Finally, I drilled all the holes on the three rail pieces *except* the holes that go into the miters; see Fig. 7. It's easier to drill these last two holes after the rail has been glued up into its final "U" shape; see Fig. 8.

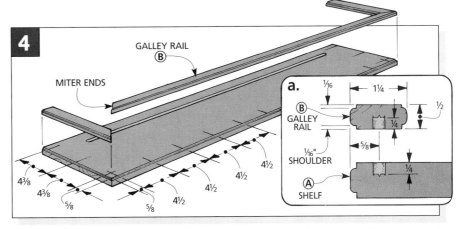

4 GALLEY RAIL Ⓑ — MITER ENDS — $4\frac{3}{8}$ $4\frac{3}{8}$ $\frac{5}{8}$ $\frac{5}{8}$ $4\frac{1}{2}$ $4\frac{1}{2}$ $4\frac{1}{2}$ $4\frac{1}{2}$ $4\frac{1}{2}$

a. $\frac{1}{16}$ $1\frac{1}{4}$ Ⓑ GALLEY RAIL $\frac{1}{2}$ $\frac{1}{4}$ $\frac{1}{16}$" SHOULDER $\frac{5}{8}$ Ⓐ SHELF $\frac{1}{4}$

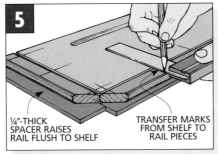

5 $\frac{1}{4}$"-THICK SPACER RAISES RAIL FLUSH TO SHELF · TRANSFER MARKS FROM SHELF TO RAIL PIECES

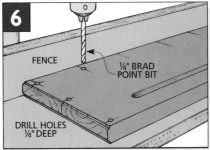

6 FENCE · $\frac{1}{4}$" BRAD POINT BIT · DRILL HOLES $\frac{1}{4}$" DEEP

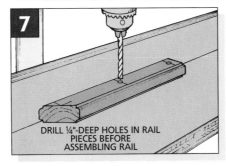

7 DRILL $\frac{1}{4}$"-DEEP HOLES IN RAIL PIECES BEFORE ASSEMBLING RAIL

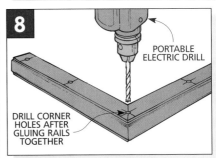

8 PORTABLE ELECTRIC DRILL · DRILL CORNER HOLES AFTER GLUING RAILS TOGETHER

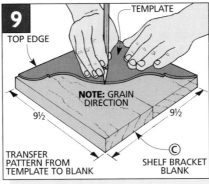

9 TEMPLATE · TOP EDGE · **NOTE:** GRAIN DIRECTION · $9\frac{1}{2}$ · $9\frac{1}{2}$ · TRANSFER PATTERN FROM TEMPLATE TO BLANK · Ⓒ SHELF BRACKET BLANK

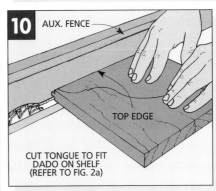

10 AUX. FENCE · TOP EDGE · CUT TONGUE TO FIT DADO ON SHELF (REFER TO FIG. 2a)

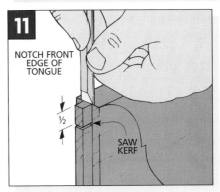

11 NOTCH FRONT EDGE OF TONGUE · $\frac{1}{2}$ · SAW KERF

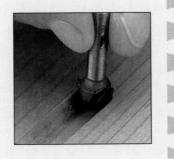

Router Bit Scraper

Occasionally when routing a profile such as the stopped plate groove on this quilt rack, I'll end up with burn marks. To remove them, I use the same router bit (removed from the router) as a scraper.

Hold the "scraper" at a slight angle. Then scrape the profile clean.

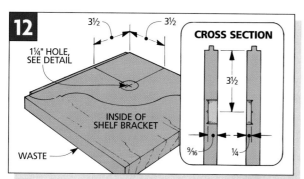

12 1¼" HOLE, SEE DETAIL · 3½ · 3½ · INSIDE OF SHELF BRACKET · WASTE

CROSS SECTION · 3½ · 9/16 · ¼

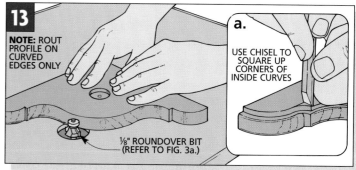

13 NOTE: ROUT PROFILE ON CURVED EDGES ONLY · 1/8" ROUNDOVER BIT (REFER TO FIG. 3a.)

a. USE CHISEL TO SQUARE UP CORNERS OF INSIDE CURVES

BRACKETS

There needs to be some way to support the shelf and also the quilt hanging rod. That's the job of the shelf brackets.

CUT TO SIZE. To make the brackets (C), first cut two square blanks to rough size; see Fig. 9 on page 9. Note: I cut the blanks so the grain would run *vertically* on the assembled rack.

PATTERN. Next, I laid out the pattern (from page 8) on the face of each blank. This can be done by drawing the pattern directly on each piece. But in case I wanted to make another quilt rack in the future, I made a template.

To do this, first cut a piece of 1/8" hardboard to the same width and length as the finished bracket. Then draw the profile on the face of the hardboard and cut out the pattern. Sand the profile smooth, then transfer the profile to each blank; see Fig. 9.

TONGUES. Before cutting the profile of the shelf brackets, I used the table saw to cut a short tongue centered on the top edge that fit snugly in the dado on the shelf; see Fig. 10.

Next, trim the front end of each tongue so the tongues are hidden when the rack is assembled; see Fig. 11.

DOWEL MORTISES. The dowel rod that holds the quilt fits in a mortise in each of the shelf brackets; see Fig. 12. (To drill these 1¼"-dia. mortises; see the box on the opposite page.)

Design Note: One mortise is deeper than the other to permit inserting and removing the rod; see Fig. 12a.

EDGE PROFILE. Now the shelf brackets can be cut to shape. Then rout a roundover with an 1/8" shoulder along the curved edge; see Fig. 13.

After routing a decorative profile on the shelf brackets, there's one little area that needs some work. At the inside curves on each bracket, I used a small chisel to square up the routed profile to match the edge profile; see Fig. 13a.

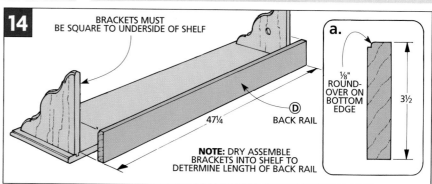

14 BRACKETS MUST BE SQUARE TO UNDERSIDE OF SHELF · 47¼ · (D) BACK RAIL · NOTE: DRY ASSEMBLE BRACKETS INTO SHELF TO DETERMINE LENGTH OF BACK RAIL

a. 1/8" ROUNDOVER ON BOTTOM EDGE · 3½

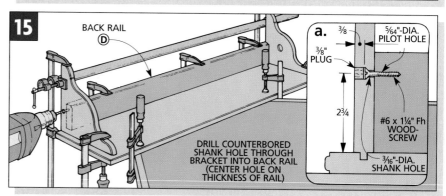

15 BACK RAIL (D) · DRILL COUNTERBORED SHANK HOLE THROUGH BRACKET INTO BACK RAIL (CENTER HOLE ON THICKNESS OF RAIL)

a. 3/8 · 3/8" PLUG · 2¾ · 5/64"-DIA. PILOT HOLE · #6 x 1¼" Fh WOOD-SCREW · 3/16"-DIA. SHANK HOLE

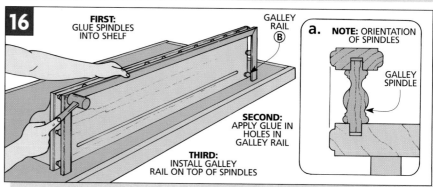

16 FIRST: GLUE SPINDLES INTO SHELF · GALLEY RAIL (B) · SECOND: APPLY GLUE IN HOLES IN GALLEY RAIL · THIRD: INSTALL GALLEY RAIL ON TOP OF SPINDLES

a. NOTE: ORIENTATION OF SPINDLES · GALLEY SPINDLE

BACK RAIL

To give the quilt rack more of a finished appearance, I added a strip of wood to the back of the rack. (It also helps tie together the shelf and the shelf brackets.)

CUT TO SIZE. First cut the back rail (D) to length to fit between the shelf brackets; see Fig. 14. As for the width of the rail, I cut it the same as the distance from the bottom of the shelf to the center of the mortise for the dowel rod.

ROUT PROFILE. Finally, rout one more profile. This time along the lower outside edge of the rail; see Fig. 14a.

ASSEMBLY. When it comes time to assemble the parts of the Quilt Rack, you need about four hands. But using several clamps and following a certain sequence works just as well.

First, dry assemble the shelf on the brackets with the back rail in between; see Fig. 14. Then temporarily clamp the parts in place; see Fig. 15.

Now, drill a counterbore for a wooden plug into the side of each bracket. Then, drill a shank hole through the bracket and a pilot hole into the rail; see Fig. 15a.

GLUE & SCREW. Next, I disassembled the pieces and started gluing. First, glue the tongues on the brackets into the dadoes in the shelf.

Then, install the back rail with glue along the upper edge of the rail and woodscrews into the ends. (Don't put glue on the ends.)

Finally, clamp everything in place and plug the screw holes.

ADD SPINDLES & RAIL. The last part of the assembly process involves gluing the spindles into the holes on top of the shelf; see Figs. 16 and 16a.

Then, glue the U-shaped galley rail onto the tops of the spindles.

DOWEL ROD & HANGER PLATES

The heart of this project is the spring-loaded rod for hanging a quilt. In order for the rod to work, the dowel must be cut to the correct length — long enough so it won't drop out of the holes, but not so long that it can't be removed.

CUT & DRILL. To determine the correct length, measure between the brackets and add $1/2$"; see Fig. 17. This way, when the dowel is inserted, it will

bottom out in the shallow ($1/4$"-deep) hole and fit $1/4$" into the deeper ($9/16$") hole in the bracket on the opposite side.

After cutting the rod to length, drill a $3/4$"-dia. mortise centered on one end for a 3"-long spring; see Fig. 17a.

Shop Note: To locate the center of this hole, I used a compass set to one-half the diameter (the radius) of the dowel; see Fig. 18. The point on the compass will leave a small hole indicating the center of the dowel.

HANGER PLATES. After gluing the spring in the mortise (I used epoxy), all that's left is to screw two hanger plates to the back of the rack; see Fig. 19.

Note: A shallow hole in the shelf will permit the screwhead to slip in behind the hanger plate; see Fig. 19a. ∎

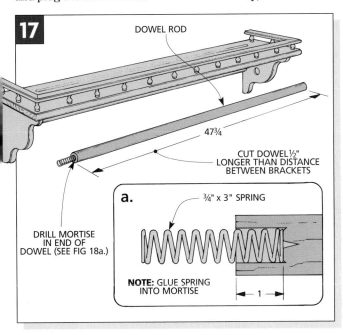

17
DOWEL ROD
47¾
CUT DOWEL ½" LONGER THAN DISTANCE BETWEEN BRACKETS
DRILL MORTISE IN END OF DOWEL (SEE FIG 18a.)

a.
¾" x 3" SPRING
NOTE: GLUE SPRING INTO MORTISE
1

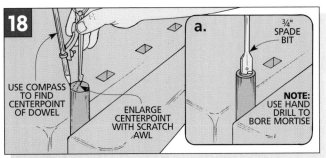

18
USE COMPASS TO FIND CENTERPOINT OF DOWEL
ENLARGE CENTERPOINT WITH SCRATCH AWL

a.
¾" SPADE BIT
NOTE: USE HAND DRILL TO BORE MORTISE

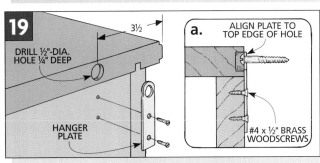

19
3½
DRILL ½"-DIA. HOLE ¼" DEEP
HANGER PLATE

a.
ALIGN PLATE TO TOP EDGE OF HOLE
#4 x ½" BRASS WOODSCREWS

Large Round Mortises

Forstner bits are ideal for drilling large flat-bottom mortises. But it can be hard to justify their cost if they're not used much. Another way to drill a large mortise is to use a hole saw and a straight router bit.

For the quilt rack, I needed to drill 1¼"-dia. shallow mortises for the quilt hanging rod. So I drilled the mortises in two steps.

The first step was to "outline" the mortise with a 1¼"-dia. hole saw; see left drawing. Then, once the mortise was established, it needed to be cleaned out.

To do this, I used my router with a ¼" straight bit; see right drawing.

Set the router bit to the same depth as the hole saw; then clean out the waste, staying within the circle cut by the hole saw.

A bit of advice though. Practice on a piece of scrap before routing the actual

workpiece. You want to make sure you have a feel for routing within the circle.

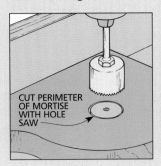

CUT PERIMETER OF MORTISE WITH HOLE SAW

¼" STRAIGHT BIT
CLEAN OUT WASTE WITH ROUTER BIT

WALL SHELVES

There isn't a single drop of glue used to hold this project together.
The trick? It's all done with sliding dovetail tongues and grooves.

The idea of assembling a whole project with dovetails may bring to mind the image of laboring for hours over a bench cutting hand-cut joints. Nothing could be farther from the truth. This project can easily be built in a weekend with a table saw and router table.

The key is that the project is assembled with dovetail tongue and groove joints. By using these you can assemble and adjust the shelves simply by sliding the pieces together. (It's sort of a "ready-to-assemble/knockdown" unit.)

This project consists of only three basic parts: the wall brackets, the shelves, and the shelf supports.

WALL BRACKETS

The wall brackets are very similar to the metal "store-bought" kind — except, in this case, they're made of ³/₄"-thick oak. Each bracket is a piece of oak 1⁵/₈" wide and 30" long with a dovetail groove cut down the center and a series of ³/₈" holes.

To make the wall brackets (A), I ripped two pieces of ³/₄"-thick oak to size; see Fig. 1. After these pieces were cut, the next step was to lay out (don't drill yet) the marks for a series of holes, 1" apart, along the entire length of the wall brackets. (These holes accept dowels that hold up the shelf supports.)

DRILL HOLES. The first holes to drill are the ones at the very top and bottom of each bracket. Since I wanted to use toggle bolts to mount the shelf to the wall, I counterbored these four holes ¹/₂" deep. Then I drilled ³/₁₆" pilot holes through these four holes only. The rest of the holes can be drilled completely through with a ³/₈" bit; see Fig. 1e.

After drilling all of the holes, I went ahead and sanded the face of the wall bracket before cutting the dovetail groove. This eliminates any danger of rounding over the edges of the groove.

DOVETAIL GROOVES. When cutting the dovetail groove, the width of the groove on the surface of the wall

EXPLODED VIEW

OVERALL DIMENSIONS:
36L x 9¾D x 30H

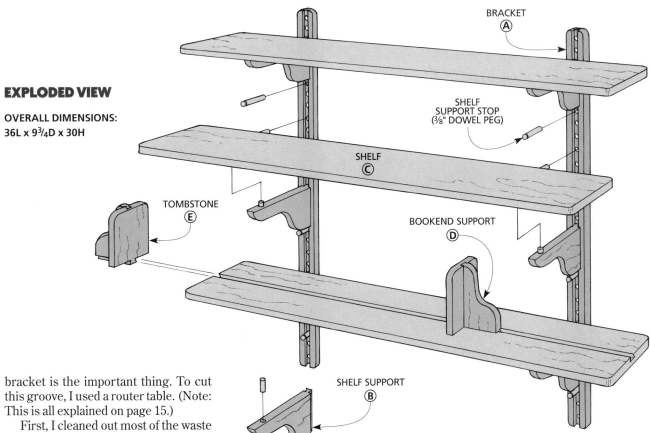

BRACKET
Ⓐ

SHELF
SUPPORT STOP
(⅜" DOWEL PEG)

SHELF
Ⓒ

TOMBSTONE
Ⓔ

BOOKEND SUPPORT
Ⓓ

SHELF SUPPORT
Ⓑ

bracket is the important thing. To cut this groove, I used a router table. (Note: This is all explained on page 15.)

First, I cleaned out most of the waste with a ¼" straight router bit; see Fig. 1a. Then I switched to a ½" dovetail bit and made two passes to cut the dovetail groove; see Figs. 1b and 1c. By making two passes, you're sure the groove is centered on the bracket, and this makes it a hair wider than ⅜" (on the surface) for a ⅜" dowel stop.

Now, sand a ½" radius on each corner; see Fig. 1e. And finally round over the front edges with a ¼" roundover bit; see Fig. 1d.

SHELF SUPPORTS

The shelves are supported by two supports which have dovetail tongues that mate with the dovetail grooves in the wall bracket. This produces a sliding joint so it's easy to adjust the height of the shelves, yet it's sturdy.

I found that the easiest way to cut the six shelf supports (B) is to use a hardboard or plywood template. First, cut the template to the shape of the support; see Fig. 2 on page 14. Then cut three pieces of stock to 3" x 12" and use the template to trace the outline of two shelf supports on each of these pieces.

The next step is to drill a ⅜" alignment hole in the top edge of each support; see Fig. 2. This hole will later accept a peg that will prevent the shelf from racking or shifting.

MATERIALS LIST - CUTTING DIAGRAM

WOOD

A	Brackets (2)	¾ x 1⅝ - 30
B	Shelf Supports (6)	¾ x 3 - 8⅜
C	Shelves (3)	¾ x 9 - 36
D	Bookend Supp. (2)	¾ x 3 - 5⅜
E	Tombstones (2)	¾ x 4 - 5

HARDWARE SUPPLIES

(1) ⅜"-dia. x 24"-long Dowel rod
(4) 3⁄16" Toggle bolts (length to fit wall thickness)

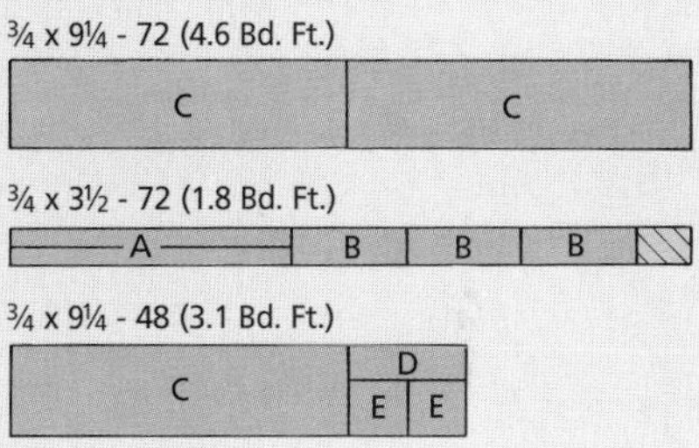

¾ x 9¼ - 72 (4.6 Bd. Ft.)

C	C

¾ x 3½ - 72 (1.8 Bd. Ft.)

A	B	B	B	

¾ x 9¼ - 48 (3.1 Bd. Ft.)

C	D	
	E	E

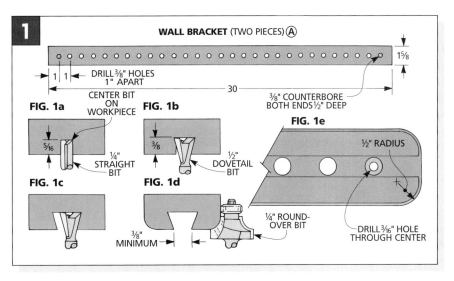

1

WALL BRACKET (TWO PIECES) Ⓐ

1⅝

DRILL ⅜" HOLES
1" APART

1 1

30

⅜" COUNTERBORE
BOTH ENDS ½" DEEP

CENTER BIT
ON
WORKPIECE

FIG. 1a

5⁄16

¼"
STRAIGHT
BIT

FIG. 1b

⅜

½"
DOVETAIL
BIT

FIG. 1e

½" RADIUS

FIG. 1c

FIG. 1d

⅜"
MINIMUM

¼" ROUND-
OVER BIT

DRILL 3⁄16" HOLE
THROUGH CENTER

Now the dovetail tongue can be cut on the back edge of each support. Using the groove in the wall bracket as a guide, cut the tongue so that it slides easily in the groove. (For more information, see opposite page.)

SHELVES

The shelves (C) are designed to be cut from a 1x10, but they can be cut and glued up from narrower strips. The final dimensions of the shelves are 9" x 36". After the shelves have been cut to size and planed flat, I softened all four corners by sanding a 1" radius on each.

PEGS

Together with the dovetail tongue and groove, the whole unit is held in place with three sets of pegs. The first set is used as stops under the shelf brackets to prevent racking.

STOPS. The shelf support stops are $3/8$" dowel, $1 1/4$" long. To make it easier to grip the stops when adjusting the shelves, I formed a knob on the end of the stops by chucking them into a drill and filing a V-groove about $3/8$" from the end; see detail in Fig. 2.

ALIGNMENT PEGS. Two more sets of pegs are attached to the shelves to prevent racking. The first set is attached to the back edge of the shelves. These pegs will fit into the dovetail grooves in the brackets; see Fig. 3.

To position the holes for these pegs, measure in 6" from each end of the shelves (this makes the holes 24" apart), and drill $3/8$" holes, $3/8$" deep. Then glue in $3/4$"-long pegs so they lock into the dovetail groove.

The second set of pegs fits in the holes in the shelf supports and lock into holes in the bottom of the shelves. To position these holes on the bottom of the shelves, square a line from the pegs already on the back edge. Then drill $3/8$" holes to align with the holes on the shelf supports. Finally, glue $3/4$"-long pegs in the shelf supports.

When the shelves are placed on the brackets, the pegs on the back edge should slide into the dovetail grooves, and the pegs on the shelf supports should mate with the holes on the bottom of the shelves.

Now there are two options: the shelves can be left the way they are, or a dovetail groove can be routed down the center for bookends as shown in Fig. 4.

BOOKENDS

The biggest hassle with book shelves is finding a way to keep the books from falling over. This is where the dovetail tongue and groove joint really comes through. A dovetail tongue is cut on the bookends (just like on the shelf brackets) so that it's loose enough to slide freely in a dovetail groove cut in the shelf. But as soon as the books start to fall over, pressure is applied to the top edge of the bookend and the dovetail tongue binds in the groove.

TOMBSTONES AND SUPPORTS. To make the bookends, I cut two "tombstones" (E) with a dovetail groove down the center; see Fig. 4. Next, two supports (D) are cut to shape (similar to the shelf supports). Then two dovetail tongues are cut on the supports. The first dovetail tongue is cut on the edge that fits in the groove in the shelf. This one can be somewhat loose.

The second dovetail tongue, though, is cut on the edge that attaches to the "tombstone." If this tongue is cut fairly tight, you might even get by without having to glue it into the support.

FINISH

I rounded over the edges of all the pieces on a router table with a $1/4$" roundover bit. Then I finished my shelves with two coats of Danish oil. (An oil finish is best on this project because it won't clog up in the dovetail grooves.) After the oil was dry, I applied a light coat of paste wax to the shoulders of the dovetail tongues so they would slide easily. ∎

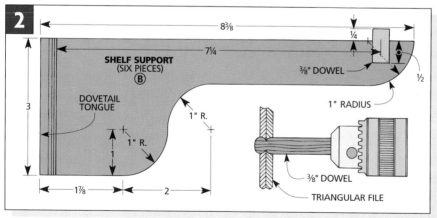

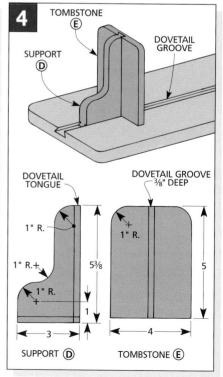

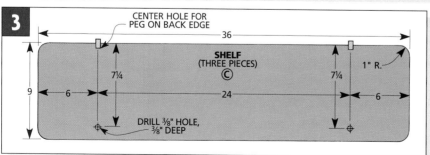

JOINERY..... *Dovetail Tongue & Groove*

Aside from its mechanical strength, the dovetail tongue and groove joint has one other feature that makes it useful: it doesn't necessarily require glue. This is especially handy if you need to create a sliding joint, as in the wall shelf. (Design Note: It's also useful in a project where you're concerned about wood expansion.)

A dovetail tongue and groove joint is fairly easy to make — provided that you have a router table in your shop. It's made by first cutting the dovetail groove (as in the wall brackets, for example). Then the dovetail tongue is cut to fit the groove.

DOVETAIL GROOVE. Since the dovetail groove must be made with only one depth setting (it cannot be made by raising the bit until the finish depth is reached, as can be done with most bits), the first step is to remove some of the waste using a $1/4$" straight bit. Set the fence so the straight bit cuts a groove in the same position as the dovetail groove

will be cut. The depth of this cut should be just a little bit less than the finished depth of the dovetail groove; see Step 1.

Now replace the $1/4$" straight bit with a $1/2$" dovetail bit, and set it for the full depth of the dovetail groove. Also move the fence very slightly farther *away* from the bit so it's offset on the workpiece; see Step 2. Then make a pass.

To center the groove on the piece, flip the board to reverse the face of the workpiece that's against the fence. Then make another pass; see Step 3.

If the groove isn't wide enough, move the fence a little farther *away* from the bit and repeat Steps 2 and 3.

DOVETAIL TONGUE. To cut the tongue, keep the dovetail bit set to the same depth setting and adjust the fence so that the bit barely cuts into the edge of a trial piece. (Be sure that the trial piece is exactly the same thickness as the actual piece.)

Then stand the piece on end, and make two passes (from right to left) on

the router table; one on each side of the board ; see Steps 4 and 5.

At this point check the size of the tongue (on the trial piece) with the dovetail groove; see Step 6. If it fits, great. Just repeat the same procedure, using the actual workpiece.

It will probably be too big to fit in the groove though. So move the fence a *little* closer to the bit. This is where a little patience pays off. Each time the fence is adjusted, make trial cuts on the scrap piece and check it with the groove to be sure that you're not cutting off too much. (Remember, each time the fence is moved, you'll actually be doubling the amount of material being removed because the cuts are made on both sides of the tongue.) Repeat the trial cuts until you obtain a good fit.

The fit of the tongue in the groove should allow the pieces to slide together without binding. But it shouldn't be so sloppy that there's a lot of side-to-side movement.

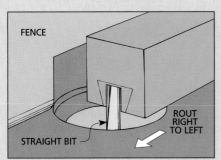

1 *Rout a groove with a $1/4$" straight bit to eliminate most of the waste wood. Set the depth of cut slightly less than the depth of the dovetail groove.*

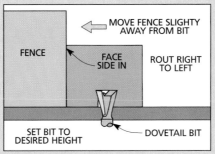

2 *Replace the $1/4$" straight bit with a $1/2$" dovetail bit. Then adjust the height of the bit and move the fence slightly farther away from the bit and make the first pass.*

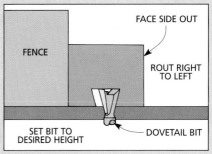

3 *To assure that the groove is centered, keep the fence and bit settings the same and make another pass, reversing the side of the piece that's facing the fence.*

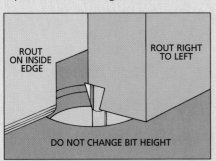

4 *To cut the tongue, keep the bit height the same and adjust the fence so that the bit makes a trial cut on a scrap piece that's the same thickness as actual piece.*

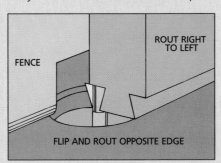

5 *Reverse the scrap and make another pass, checking it with the groove to see if too much has been removed. Then repeat Steps 4 and 5 with the actual piece.*

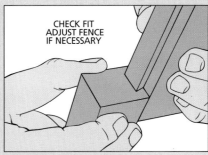

6 *After the tongue is cut on the actual piece, check it for fit with the groove. If the tongue's too large, repeat Steps 4 and 5 until it fits the groove.*

COUNTRY SHELF

This shelf has a built-in glove box. And that creates the woodworking challenge — fitting a door to leave a uniform gap all around.

One trick to building this country shelf is fitting the door. How do you end up with a uniform gap around each side? I started with the gap at the bottom — it's determined by the depth of the hinge mortises. Then after the bottom gap is established, creating the other gaps is just a matter of cutting the door to size.

HANGING SYSTEM. Another interesting challenge is figuring out how to hang this country shelf. Instead of screwing it directly to the wall, the back is beveled and hangs on a mating cleat; see the box on page 19. It's easy to position but still very strong.

FINISH. I built two shelves, one of oak (shown in the photo above) and one of pine (see the box on page 20). The oak one was finished with General Finishes' Royal Finish. To give the pine one a rustic look, I added square pegs and painted it with milk paint.

ENDS

The best place to start working on this country shelf is to make the ends (A). Begin by cutting two end blanks roughly 8½" wide. (Note: If you can't find flat stock this wide, edge glue a couple of boards together.) Then I cut them to a finished length of 16"; see Fig. 1.

CUT DADOES. The shelves fit into ¼"-deep dadoes cut in the blanks; see Fig. 1b. The width of the dadoes should match the thickness of the stock. Position the first dado 5½" from the bottom edge, the second 10½".

CUT RABBETS. After cutting the da-does, cut the rabbets for the back pieces. Like the dadoes, the rabbets should match the thickness of the stock. They're cut along the inside back edge of each blank; see Fig. 1a.

The next step is to cut the end blanks to finished width (8¼"); see Fig. 1. Doing this after cutting the dadoes cleans up any chipout. Just be sure that you trim off the front — not the rabbeted edges.

SCREW HOLES. To screw the shelves to the ends, you'll need to drill counterbores. They're centered on the width of each dado; see Fig. 1 and 1b. Then, drill shank holes through each of the counterbores.

CUT OUT SHAPE. This project gets much of its country appeal from its curved edges. To cut an identical shape

EXPLODED VIEW

OVERALL DIMENSIONS:
36L x 9D x 16H

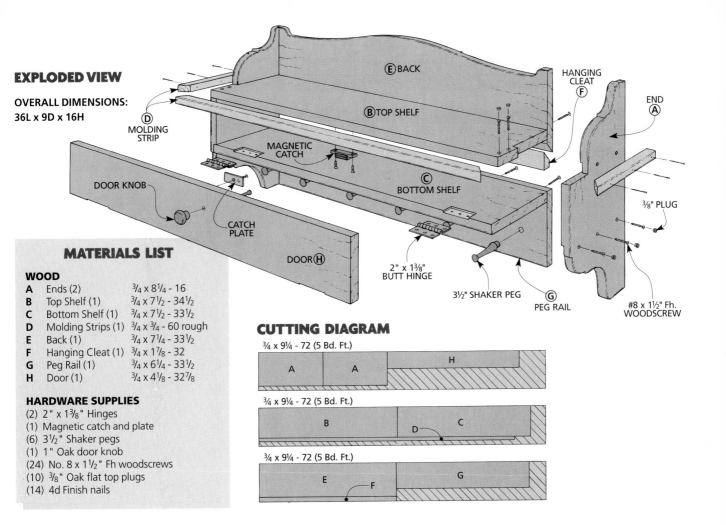

(E) BACK
(B) TOP SHELF
(F) HANGING CLEAT
END (A)
(D) MOLDING STRIP
MAGNETIC CATCH
(C) BOTTOM SHELF
³⁄₈" PLUG
DOOR KNOB
CATCH PLATE
DOOR (H)
2" x 1³⁄₈" BUTT HINGE
3½" SHAKER PEG
(G) PEG RAIL
#8 x 1½" Fh. WOODSCREW

MATERIALS LIST

WOOD

A	Ends (2)	³⁄₄ x 8¹⁄₄ - 16
B	Top Shelf (1)	³⁄₄ x 7¹⁄₂ - 34¹⁄₂
C	Bottom Shelf (1)	³⁄₄ x 7¹⁄₂ - 33¹⁄₂
D	Molding Strips (1)	³⁄₄ x ³⁄₄ - 60 rough
E	Back (1)	³⁄₄ x 7¹⁄₄ - 33¹⁄₂
F	Hanging Cleat (1)	³⁄₄ x 1⁷⁄₈ - 32
G	Peg Rail (1)	³⁄₄ x 6¹⁄₄ - 33¹⁄₂
H	Door (1)	³⁄₄ x 4¹⁄₈ - 32⁷⁄₈

HARDWARE SUPPLIES

(2) 2" x 1³⁄₈" Hinges
(1) Magnetic catch and plate
(6) 3½" Shaker pegs
(1) 1" Oak door knob
(24) No. 8 x 1½" Fh woodscrews
(10) ³⁄₈" Oak flat top plugs
(14) 4d Finish nails

CUTTING DIAGRAM

³⁄₄ x 9¹⁄₄ - 72 (5 Bd. Ft.)

A | A | H

³⁄₄ x 9¹⁄₄ - 72 (5 Bd. Ft.)

B | D | C

³⁄₄ x 9¹⁄₄ - 72 (5 Bd. Ft.)

E | F | G

on both ends, I taped them together with double-sided carpet tape (dadoes facing in).

Now lay out the curved pattern on one face of the end pieces and cut just a little bit outside the lines; see Fig. 2. Then, to smooth up to the lines, I used a drum sander.

ROUND OVER EDGES. To complete the two ends and to give the whole project a softer appearance, I routed a ¹⁄₄" roundover on all the edges except the back edge. Note: To prevent any gaps where the shelves meet the ends, some of the edges and back edge aren't rounded over; see Fig. 2a.

SHELVES

With the ends complete, I began on the shelves that form the top and bottom of the "glove box." The top shelf is a little different. It has molding strips along the front and sides, so it looks like it extends *through* the ends; refer to Fig. 6.

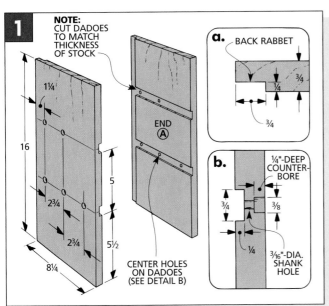

1

NOTE: CUT DADOES TO MATCH THICKNESS OF STOCK

END (A)

1¹⁄₄
16
2³⁄₄
8¹⁄₄
5
2³⁄₄
5¹⁄₂

CENTER HOLES ON DADOES (SEE DETAIL B)

a. BACK RABBET
³⁄₄ | ¹⁄₄ | ³⁄₄

b. ¹⁄₄"-DEEP COUNTER-BORE
³⁄₄ | ³⁄₈
¹⁄₄
³⁄₁₆"-DIA. SHANK HOLE

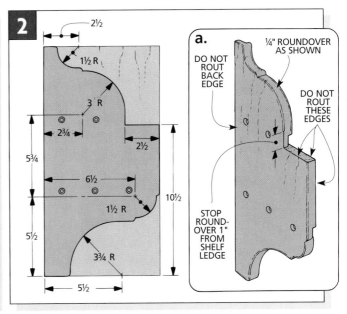

2

2¹⁄₂
1¹⁄₂ R
3 R
2³⁄₄
2¹⁄₂
5³⁄₄
6¹⁄₂
10¹⁄₂
1¹⁄₂ R
5¹⁄₂
3³⁄₄ R
5¹⁄₂

a. ¹⁄₄" ROUNDOVER AS SHOWN
DO NOT ROUT BACK EDGE
DO NOT ROUT THESE EDGES
STOP ROUND-OVER 1" FROM SHELF LEDGE

COUNTRY SHELF   **17**

Cut To Size. To find the width of the top shelf (B) and bottom shelf (C), measure the length of the lower dado on the ends (A); see Fig. 3. (Start from the shoulder of the back rabbet.) Then rip both shelves to this width.

Next, cut the bottom shelf (C) to length ($33\frac{1}{2}$"); see Fig. 4. Then clamp the shelf between the two ends and measure from the outside face of one end to the outside of the other. This will be the length of the top shelf (B) ($34\frac{1}{2}$" in my case); see Fig. 3.

Top Shelf. With the shelves cut to size, set the bottom shelf aside. The top shelf extends across the front edge of each end, so cut a notch out of the back corners; see Fig. 3. The length of this notch equals the length of the top dado in the ends (A). (Again, measure from the shoulder of the back rabbet.)

At this point, I drilled the pilot holes for the magnetic door catch; see Fig. 3. Inset the door catch a distance equal to the thickness of the stock *plus* the catch plate. To do this, I stuck the plate to the door catch and positioned them $\frac{3}{4}$" in from the front edge.

Bottom Shelf. Next, I went back to the bottom shelf. First, lay out the locations of the mortises for the hinges; see Fig. 4.

I wanted a uniform $\frac{1}{16}$" gap around the door. If the hinges were mounted flush with the surface, the gap between the shelf and the door would be about $\frac{1}{8}$". So I cut the mortise on the shelf a little deeper — to half the thickness of the hinge barrel; see Fig. 4a.

After the mortises are cut, drill pilot holes for the screws. Then, rout a $\frac{1}{4}$" roundover on the front bottom edge; see Fig. 4a.

Assembly. At this point, dry assemble the shelves (B and C) and ends (A), and mark the position of the pilot holes on the shelves; see Fig. 5. After drilling the holes, glue and screw the shelves between the ends.

To prevent the top shelf from cupping at the front, I also drilled and screwed the shelf to the ends from the top; see Fig. 5 and 5a. Then I plugged all the screw holes except those covered by the molding strips.

Molding. The molding strips cover the edges of the top shelf. (The thicknesses of the strips should match the thickness of the shelf.) I started by

rounding over the front edges of the $\frac{3}{4}$"-wide molding strips (D); see Fig. 6. Then I cut one 40"-long strip, plus two 10"-long strips.

For the molding to fit best at the mitered corners, I cut the front piece first so the distance between the short points equals the length of the top shelf; see Fig. 6.

After the front strip is glued on, miter the other strips to fit on the sides. But only apply glue to the *front* ends of these strips. This allows for expansion and contraction with changes in humidity. Then nail the strips on and set the nails; see Fig. 6.

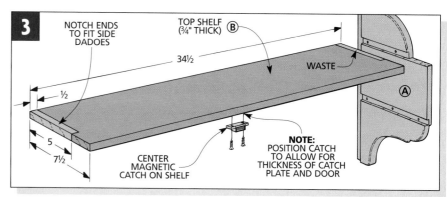

3 NOTCH ENDS TO FIT SIDE DADOES — TOP SHELF (B) ($\frac{3}{4}$" THICK) — WASTE — $34\frac{1}{2}$ — $\frac{1}{2}$ — 5 — $7\frac{1}{2}$ — CENTER MAGNETIC CATCH ON SHELF — **NOTE:** POSITION CATCH TO ALLOW FOR THICKNESS OF CATCH PLATE AND DOOR — Ⓐ

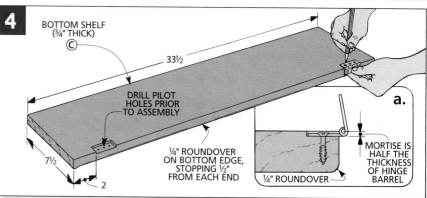

4 BOTTOM SHELF ($\frac{3}{4}$" THICK) Ⓒ — $33\frac{1}{2}$ — DRILL PILOT HOLES PRIOR TO ASSEMBLY — $7\frac{1}{2}$ — 2 — $\frac{1}{4}$" ROUNDOVER ON BOTTOM EDGE, STOPPING $\frac{1}{2}$" FROM EACH END — **a.** — MORTISE IS HALF THE THICKNESS OF HINGE BARREL — $\frac{1}{4}$" ROUNDOVER

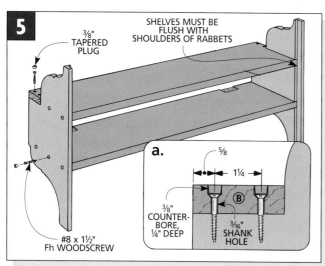

5 $\frac{3}{8}$" TAPERED PLUG — SHELVES MUST BE FLUSH WITH SHOULDERS OF RABBETS — **a.** — $\frac{5}{8}$ — $1\frac{1}{4}$ — Ⓑ — $\frac{3}{8}$" COUNTERBORE, $\frac{1}{4}$" DEEP — $\frac{3}{16}$" SHANK HOLE — #8 x $1\frac{1}{2}$" Fh WOODSCREW

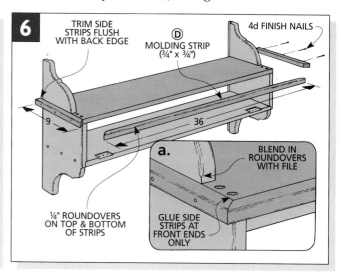

6 TRIM SIDE STRIPS FLUSH WITH BACK EDGE — Ⓓ MOLDING STRIP ($\frac{3}{4}$" x $\frac{3}{4}$") — 4d FINISH NAILS — 9 — 36 — **a.** — $\frac{1}{4}$" ROUNDOVERS ON TOP & BOTTOM OF STRIPS — BLEND IN ROUNDOVERS WITH FILE — GLUE SIDE STRIPS AT FRONT ENDS ONLY

BACKS

The back of this project is different than you might expect. Instead of one wide piece, it has two — a back (E) at the top and a peg rail (G) at the bottom. The gap between the pieces allows the country shelf to hang on a cleat that's screwed to the wall; see the box at right.

CUT BACK. The cleat is originally part of the back (E). Start by ripping the piece to a rough width of $9\frac{1}{4}$". Then cut the back piece to length so it will fit between the rabbets in the ends (A); see Fig. 8. (In my case, $33\frac{1}{2}$" long.) Then, I tilted the table saw blade to 45° and ripped the back to a width of $7\frac{1}{4}$". Keep the waste piece. It will be used later as the hanging cleat (F).

CUT CURVE. The next step is to lay out the curve on the *back* side of the back (E); see Figs. 7 and 8. Mark the centerline on the workpiece and transfer the half-pattern to it. Then flip the pattern over and transfer it to the other half of the workpiece. Now, with a band saw or sabre saw, cut out the curve, staying $\frac{1}{16}$" from the line. Finally, I used a drum sander to smooth up to the line.

Hanging System

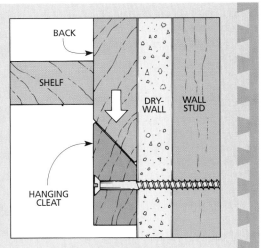

Here's how the hanging system works. A beveled cleat is cut to length so it fits easily into the opening between the ends of the country shelf. Then the cleat is screwed to a pair of studs in the wall. After it's finished, the shelf is hung on the cleat so the mating bevels interlock. (Note: You could easily adapt this same system for other shelves or wall-hung cabinets.)

CUT PEG RAIL. Now the peg rail (G) is cut to size. To determine the width of this piece, measure from the top edge of the bottom shelf to the bottom of the end pieces ($6\frac{1}{4}$"); see Figs. 9 and 10. Like the back (E), it fits between the rabbets ($33\frac{1}{2}$" long).

DRILL PEG HOLES. After the peg rail is cut to size, drill holes for the Shaker pegs; see Fig. 9. These holes are centered on a line drawn $2\frac{3}{4}$" from the bottom edge. Begin the series of holes with a hole centered 3" from the end. Then drill the remaining five holes at $5\frac{1}{2}$" intervals (center to center).

ROUT ROUNDOVERS. Before attaching both the back and the peg rail, I routed a $\frac{1}{4}$" roundover along the upper front edge of the back (E); see Fig. 8a. I also routed the lower front edge of the peg rail (G); see Fig. 9. (Note: To prevent any gaps where these pieces fit into the rabbets, stop the roundovers $\frac{1}{2}$" from the end of each piece.)

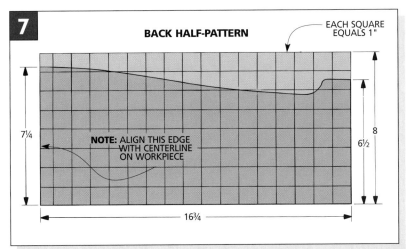

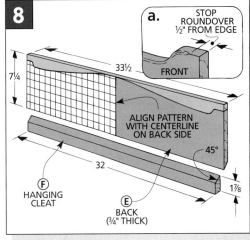

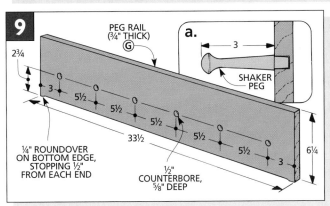

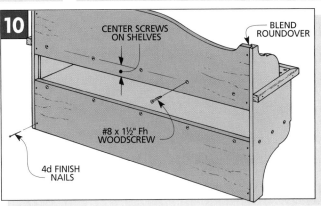

ATTACH BACKS. Now, drill countersunk screw holes through the back and the peg rail and into the shelves; see Fig. 10. Then screw these pieces to the shelves. To hold the back and peg rail in tight, I also nailed them into the rabbets. (Shop Note: To avoid splitting the wood, I drilled pilot holes and used 4d finish nails, angling them slightly.)

BLEND ROUNDOVERS. Some of the roundovers on the ends (A) and back pieces (E and G) were stopped short so there wouldn't be gaps at the joints. But now that these pieces are assembled, you can finish rounding them over. Unfortunately, your router won't work in some places, so use a file to blend the roundovers; see Figs. 6a and 10.

DOOR

All that's left is the door. It should have a consistent gap around each edge. To get this, I cut the door to fit tight and trimmed it for an even gap later.

CUT DOOR. Start by measuring the opening and cut the door (H) to fit. Then rip it 1/16" narrower than the height of the opening so you can close the door when the hinges are mounted.

Now, attach the hinges to the bottom shelf with a "stubby" screwdriver. Then, to mark the position of the hinges, clamp them to the door; see Fig. 11. Note: The door should be centered across the opening.

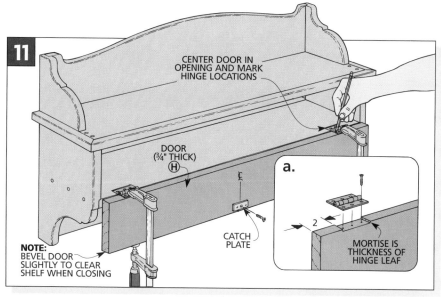

11 CENTER DOOR IN OPENING AND MARK HINGE LOCATIONS

DOOR (¾" THICK) (H)

a.

2

MORTISE IS THICKNESS OF HINGE LEAF

CATCH PLATE

NOTE: BEVEL DOOR SLIGHTLY TO CLEAR SHELF WHEN CLOSING

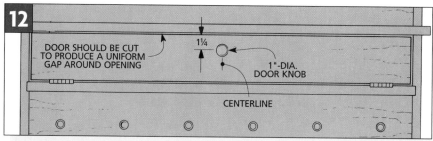

12 DOOR SHOULD BE CUT TO PRODUCE A UNIFORM GAP AROUND OPENING

1¼

1"-DIA. DOOR KNOB

CENTERLINE

CUT MORTISES. Next, cut the hinge mortises on the edge of the door; see Fig. 11a. Since the mortises in the shelf determined the gap along the bottom, these mortises can be cut to the thickness of the hinge leaf.

TRIM DOOR. After screwing the hinges to the door, measure the gap along the bottom and mark the top and sides so they'll have uniform gaps. Then remove the door and trim the top and sides.

HARDWARE. Finally, drill pilot holes for the catch plate and door knob; see Figs. 11 and 12. Then apply finish to the shelf and mount the hardware. ■

Aging Techniques

On the country shelf that I made out of pine I wanted to add a hundred years to the appearance. To do this, I included some different details.

Instead of round plugs, I covered the screws in the ends and the top with traditional square pegs; see below.

Then, to finish the pine, I used what a country craftsman may have used — milk paint. (It's available from many mail order catalogs; see page 95.)

Finally I distressed the wood. Adding dings can make a project look aged, but be careful — it can be overdone.

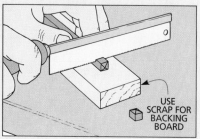

1 To make square pegs, first cut a 3/8"-square piece about 18" long. Then, using a disk sander, shape end to a pyramid and cut peg about 3/8" long.

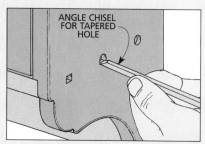

ANGLE CHISEL FOR TAPERED HOLE

2 Next, square the screw holes with a chisel. The pegs fit easy if you round their bottom edges with sandpaper. Finally, add glue and tap in the pegs.

To give the country shelf a worn appearance, sand some edges after painting, and round corners to show wear. Then add dents and scratches.

WALL CUPBOARD

The challenge in designing this project was to figure a way to build a solid wood back panel that could "move" with changes in humidity.

I f your family is like mine, you've probably acquired a number of family heirlooms. My collection includes the plate my grandmother traditionally used to serve the Thanksgiving turkey, a set of good china, and some figurines that belonged to my great aunt. I finally decided these heirlooms needed a home of their own.

SIDES

To build the cupboard, I started with the sides (A). Glue up enough $^3/_4$" stock to get two blanks with rough dimensions of $10^1/_2$" wide by 31" long. After these blanks are dry and planed flat, trim them to final size; see Fig. 1.

STOPPED DADOES. The two side pieces are joined to the three shelves with tongue and dado joints. This means three $^1/_4$"-wide by $^3/_8$"-deep dadoes are routed in both side pieces.

First, mark the centerlines and "stop" points on the three dadoes; see Fig. 1. To rout the dadoes and keep them aligned across both sides, I clamped the two pieces together, back edge to back edge (bookmatch style), and then routed the dadoes across both side pieces at the same time; refer to page 27.

SIDE PROFILES. After the dadoes are routed, the profile on the sides can be laid out. Start by locating the six centerpoints to draw the six arcs on one of the side pieces; see Fig. 2.

The small radius arcs (at points A, B, D, and F) can be drawn with a standard pencil compass. But to draw the two large arcs (at points C and E) I used a beam compass.

Shop Note: A beam compass is just a thin strip of wood with a notch at one end to cradle the point of a pencil. Then a $^1/_{16}$" hole is drilled along the "beam" wherever a pivot point is needed. Insert a brad in this hole and pivot the beam

around it to draw the large radius arcs.

After the six arcs are drawn, you have to draw some connecting curves to complete the profile.

CUT OUT PROFILE. Before cutting the profile, I used a hole saw to drill the holes at points D and F to form the $^3/_4$"-radiuses ($1^1/_2$" diameter). Then cut the rest of the profile using a sabre saw or band saw.

Shop Note: Just to be on the safe side, I found it was best to cut about $^1/_{16}$" outside of the marked profile. Then I used a drum sander on the drill press to sand down to the marked lines.

CUT SECOND SIDE. After the first side piece is sanded, use it as a template to mark the other side piece. Then cut and sand it to size.

SHELVES

Next, the three shelves are cut to size. Rip the top shelf (B) to a width of $4^1/_2$", and the middle and bottom shelves (C) to a width of 7". Then cut all three to final length ($35^3/_4$"); see Fig. 3.

CUT TONGUES. After the shelves are cut to size, a tongue is cut on each end to fit the dadoes in the side pieces. (Again, see pages 27 and 28 for more.)

After the tongues are cut to fit snugly in the dadoes, notch each tongue $^1/_2$" back from the front edge; see Fig. 3a. (This notch serves two purposes. First, it provides a neat-looking joint line on the front corner of the shelf. It also allows the shelf to be pushed forward $^1/_2$" to permit room for the back panel.)

OVERALL DIMENSIONS: 36½W x 9D x 30⅞H

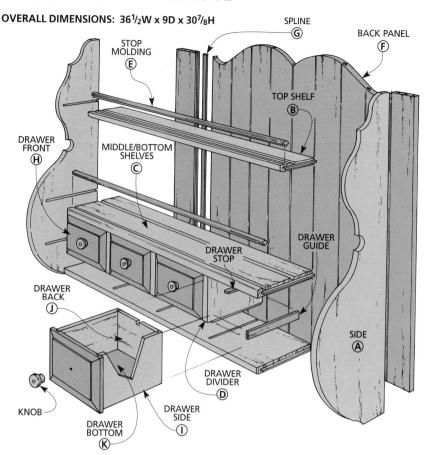

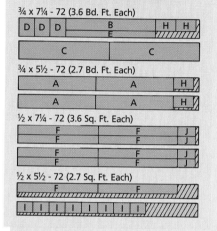

MATERIALS LIST

A	Sides (2)	¾ x 9 - 29½
B	Top Shelf (1)	¾ x 4½ - 35¾
C	Mid./Bot. Shelv. (2)	¾ x 7 - 35¾
D	Drawer Dividers (3)	¾ x 7 - 5¼
E	Stop Moldings (2)	¾ x ¾ - 35
F	Bk. Panel Pcs. (10)	½ x 3½ - 32
G	Splines	cut from waste
H	Drawer Fronts (4)	¾ x 4⁷⁄₁₆ - 8⅛
I	Drawer Sides (8)	½ x 4⁷⁄₁₆ - 6½
J	Drawer Backs (4)	½ x 3½ - 7⅛
K	Drawer Btms. (4)	¼ ply (cut to fit)

HARDWARE SUPPLIES

(24) No. 8 x 1" Fh woodscrews
(4) 1¼" Maple knobs with brass centers
(2) Brass hangers with screws

CUTTING DIAGRAM

¾ x 7¼ - 72 (3.6 Bd. Ft. Each)

½ x 7¼ - 72 (3.6 Sq. Ft. Each)

¾ x 5½ - 72 (2.7 Bd. Ft. Each)

½ x 5½ - 72 (2.7 Sq. Ft. Each)

STOP MOLDING GROOVE. After the tongues are cut, ¼" grooves are routed on the top and middle shelves for stop moldings that are mounted near the *front edge* of the shelves; see Fig. 4. (The grooves are routed now, but the stop moldings aren't added until later; refer to Fig. 14.)

PLATE GROOVE. Next, a plate groove is routed on the same sides of these two pieces. (This rounded groove holds plates upright for display.) To make this groove, use a ½" core box bit on the router table; see Fig. 5. Center the groove 2½" from the *back edge*.

DADOES FOR DIVIDERS. To complete the shelves, stopped dadoes are routed for the three dividers (D) that are mounted between the middle and bottom shelves.

To locate these dadoes, start with the middle dado. First, measure the distance between the shoulders on the ends of the shelves and mark a line centered on this distance to locate the middle dado; see Fig. 6.

Then to determine the location of the other two dadoes, I had to do a little math. (In order to get equal spacing be-

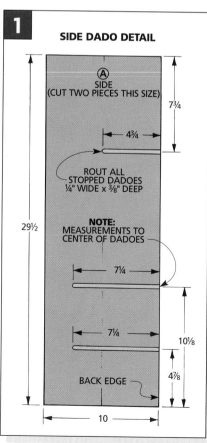

1 SIDE DADO DETAIL

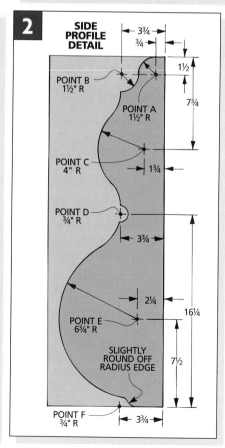

2 SIDE PROFILE DETAIL

tween the dividers, the dadoes do not lay out in equal increments.)

To get the right spacing, take the distance between the shoulders of the shelf (this should be 35") and divide this distance by four (to get $8\frac{3}{4}$").

Then add one-fourth the thickness of the drawer dividers (D) to this distance. (I divided $\frac{3}{4}$" by 4 to get $\frac{3}{16}$". I added this to $8\frac{3}{4}$" for a total of $8\frac{15}{16}$".)

This is the distance from the *center* of the middle stopped dado to the *center* of the other two stopped dadoes; see Fig. 6. (Note that the remaining distance is only $8\frac{9}{16}$" from the middle of these dadoes to the shoulders at the ends of the shelves. This is the correct distance to get equal spacing when the dividers are in place.)

After marking the centerlines of the three dadoes, clamp the two shelves together (back edge to back edge) and use the same technique as on the sides to rout the stopped dadoes.

DRAWER DIVIDERS

After the dadoes are routed, the three drawer dividers (D) can be cut to fit. (Note: Since the dividers are mounted so the grain runs vertically, the length is shorter than the width; see Fig. 8.)

DETERMINING THE LENGTH. To determine the length of the dividers, first dry clamp the middle and bottom shelves to the side pieces. Then measure the distance between the two shelves to get the shoulder-to-shoulder distance of the dividers; see Fig. 7.

To this measurement, add the depth of the two dadoes to allow for the tongues on the dividers. (In my case, this came to a length of $5\frac{1}{4}$".) Now cut the dividers to this length and the same width as the shelves (7"); see Fig. 8.

CUTTING THE TONGUES. Next, cut tongues centered on both ends to fit the dadoes in the shelves.

Then notch the front edge of each tongue to fit the stopped dado so the front edge of the divider rests flush with the front edge of the shelves; see Fig. 9.

DRAWER STOP HOLES. There's one thing you need to do now. Drawer stops are added to the bottom of the middle shelf *after* assembly (refer to Fig. 30), but the holes for these stops have to be drilled *now*; see Fig. 10. If you don't drill these holes now, you won't be able to fit the drill between the shelves later. Each hole is centered on a drawer opening.

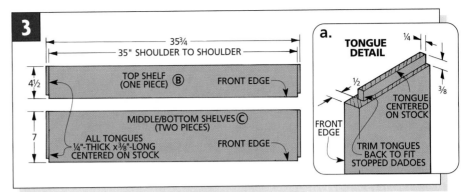

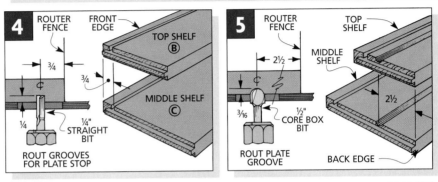

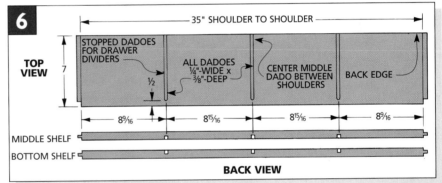

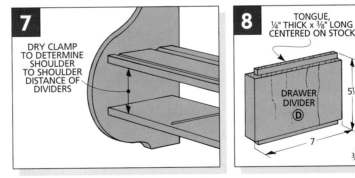

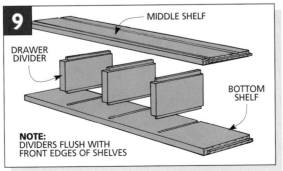

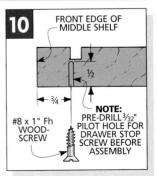

STOP MOLDING

To complete the shelves, I cut the two stop moldings (E) that fit in the grooves routed in the top and middle shelves.

To make these moldings, cut rabbets on all four edges of a piece of ³/₄" stock, creating tongues to fit the grooves in the shelves; see Fig. 11. After the tongues are cut, rip ³/₄"-wide molding strips off each edge.

ROUNDOVER EDGES. Now the top edges of the strips can be rounded to a partial bullnose profile with a ³/₈" roundover bit; see Fig. 11a.

Before assembling the pieces, I used the same setup to round over both front edges of the side pieces and the top shelf, the top front edge of the middle shelf, and the bottom front edge of the bottom shelf; see Fig. 14a.

ASSEMBLY. At last, everything is ready for assembly. Start by gluing the dividers between the middle and bottom shelves, making sure that the ends are square; see Fig. 12.

When the shelf/divider unit is dry, glue this unit and the top shelf between the sides. As these pieces are clamped, be sure to push the shelves forward enough to leave room for the ¹/₂"-thick back panel. To get uniform spacing, place a ¹/₂"-thick spacer block between each shelf and the clamp; see Fig. 13.

Finally, cut the stop moldings to fit between the sides and glue them into the grooves in the shelves; see Fig. 14.

BACK PANEL

To complete the cupboard, I made a back panel out of 10 individual boards. Start by cutting eight pieces of ¹/₂" stock 3¹/₂" wide by 32" long. Then cut two more pieces an extra ¹/₈" wide (3⁵/₈" wide) for the two outside pieces. (These pieces are trimmed to fit later.)

CHAMFER & GROOVE EDGES. Next, rout a ¹/₁₆" chamfer on both edges of the face (front) side of the first eight pieces, but only one edge of the two outside pieces; see Fig. 16.

All of these back pieces are joined together with splines. To do this, first cut a ¹/₈"-wide groove centered on both edges of each piece; see Fig. 17. (On the two outside pieces, cut the groove only in the edges with the chamfer.)

SPLINES. Now, rip ¹/₈"-thick splines (G) off the edge of a piece of ³/₄"-thick stock; see Fig. 18.

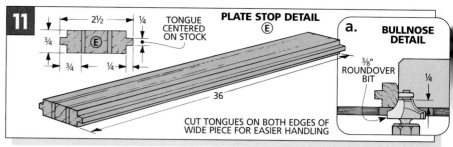

11 PLATE STOP DETAIL — 2¹/₂ — ¹/₄ — TONGUE CENTERED ON STOCK — ³/₄ — (E) — ³/₄ — ¹/₄ — 36 — CUT TONGUES ON BOTH EDGES OF WIDE PIECE FOR EASIER HANDLING

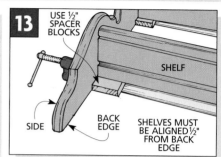

a. BULLNOSE DETAIL — ³/₈" ROUNDOVER BIT — ¹/₄

12 CLAMP AND CHECK SHELF ENDS FOR SQUARE

13 USE ¹/₂" SPACER BLOCKS — SHELF — SIDE — BACK EDGE — SHELVES MUST BE ALIGNED ¹/₂" FROM BACK EDGE

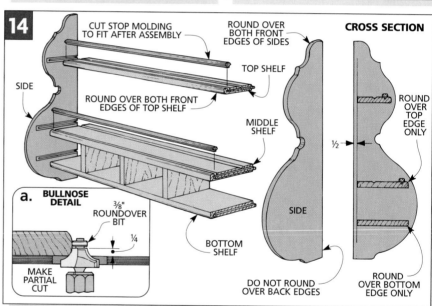

14 CUT STOP MOLDING TO FIT AFTER ASSEMBLY — ROUND OVER BOTH FRONT EDGES OF SIDES — TOP SHELF — SIDE — ROUND OVER BOTH FRONT EDGES OF TOP SHELF — MIDDLE SHELF — BOTTOM SHELF — DO NOT ROUND OVER BACK EDGES — CROSS SECTION — ROUND OVER TOP EDGE ONLY — ¹/₂ — SIDE — ROUND OVER BOTTOM EDGE ONLY

a. BULLNOSE DETAIL — ³/₈" ROUNDOVER BIT — ¹/₄ — MAKE PARTIAL CUT

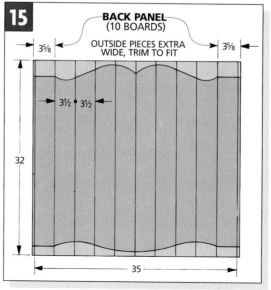

15 BACK PANEL (10 BOARDS) — 3⁵/₈ — OUTSIDE PIECES EXTRA WIDE, TRIM TO FIT — 3⁵/₈ — 3¹/₂ — 3¹/₂ — 32 — 35

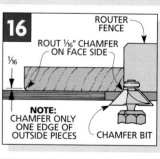

16 ROUTER FENCE — ROUT ¹/₁₆" CHAMFER ON FACE SIDE — ¹/₁₆ — NOTE: CHAMFER ONLY ONE EDGE OF OUTSIDE PIECES — CHAMFER BIT

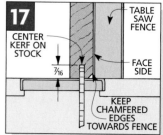

17 TABLE SAW FENCE — CENTER KERF ON STOCK — ⁷/₁₆ — FACE SIDE — KEEP CHAMFERED EDGES TOWARDS FENCE

Then glue each spline into *only one groove* of each back piece; see Fig. 19.

Design Note: Since the boards are unsupported at the top and bottom, the splines keep the faces of the boards flush — preventing them from twisting forward or backward. However, they're glued into only one groove to allow for expansion and contraction. (For more on wood movement, see the box below.)

CUT BACK TO FIT. Now, place the back pieces between the two sides on the assembled wall cupboard. The combined width should be too wide to fit, so trim the two outside pieces until they fit between the sides.

TEMPLATES. To complete the back panel, curves are cut on the top and bottom edges; see Fig. 22. To cut the curves, I made two templates. Tape a piece of poster board to the edge of the workbench and draw a 6"-radius and a 3¼"-radius arc to form the top profile; see Fig. 20. (Actually this is only half of the profile, just flip the template over to trace the other half.)

Follow the same procedure to draw a 26"-radius and a 10"-radius arc for the profile on the bottom edge; see Fig. 21.

CUT THE PROFILE. Now clamp the back panel pieces together and use the templates to mark the profiles. After they're marked, cut the edges to shape with a sabre saw. Then sand the edges smooth and rout a 1/16" chamfer on the top and bottom face (front) edges.

ATTACH THE BACK. At this point the back panel pieces can be fastened down by drilling countersunk pilot holes centered on the width of each back piece; see Fig. 23. Then screw the back pieces in place with No. 8 x 1" flathead screws.

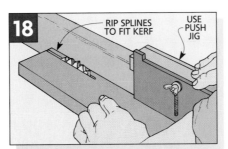

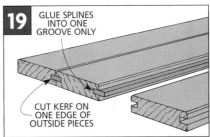

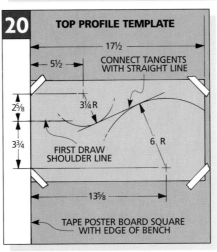

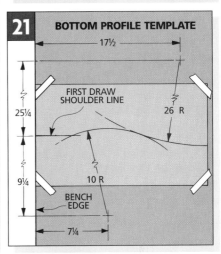

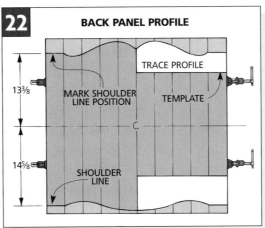

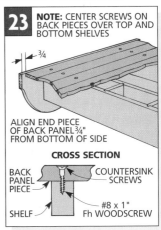

Wood Movement

Every time you use solid wood for a project, you have to be aware of wood movement — the expansion and contraction of wood during seasonal changes in humidity.

When the humidity is high, wood (even a piece with finish on it) absorbs moisture from the air and expands. Then when the humidity is low, wood releases moisture and contracts.

How much does wood move? As a general rule of thumb you can count on kiln-dried wood (at about 7% moisture content) moving about 1/8" per 12" in width, or about 1%.

Wood movement was a major consideration when I was designing the wall cupboard. I was concerned with the wood expanding and buckling the pieces at each joint.

I built this project in the summer, so the wood was already at its widest on the expansion/contraction cycle. As I mounted the boards, I pushed them together with light pressure. However, if I had built this project in the winter, I would have laid out the boards to allow for summertime expansion.

Using the 1% rule of thumb, there should be about a 1/32"-gap between each 3½"-wide board. The easiest way to gauge this gap is with playing cards. The combined thickness of three playing cards is within a few thousandths of 1/32".

As the boards are mounted, place three cards between each of the joints. This should provide adequate spacing for the wood to swell during the humid summer months.

DRAWERS

After the back panel is screwed in place, the last step is to build the drawers. Start work on the drawers by cutting the four fronts (H) from ³/₄" stock so they're ¹/₁₆" less than the width and length of the drawer openings. Then cut eight sides (I) out of ¹/₂" stock to the same width as the fronts and 6¹/₂" long.

JOINERY. The drawer fronts and sides are joined with dovetail tongue and groove joints. (For more on this joint, see page 15.) First cut dovetail grooves on the back of the drawer front, using a ¹/₄" dovetail bit; see Fig. 25.

Next, keep the bit at the same height and move the fence to rout a tongue on one end of each drawer side; see Fig. 26.

To hold the plywood bottom (K), rout straight grooves on the inside of the sides and front; see Fig. 24a. Rout through grooves in the sides. But in the front, start and stop the groove at the dovetail grooves; see Fig. 24.

RAISED FRONT. After the joints were cut, I used a Sears Panel Raising Bit (No. 25465) to cut a beveled border on each drawer front; see Fig. 28.

BACK. Next the back (J) can be cut to size. To determine its length, dry assemble the drawer and measure between the sides; see Fig. 27. Then add ¹/₂" for the tongues and cut the backs to this length and a rough width of 4".

Now cut the tongue and dado joints to join the back to the sides; see Fig. 29.

Next, cut the bottoms (K) out of ¹/₄" plywood to fit, and slide them in place. Then cut the back to finished width so it's flush with the top of the sides.

Also, before gluing up the drawer, cut a notch on the top edge of the back for the drawer stop; see Fig. 27.

DRAWER STOPS. The drawer stops are simply small wooden turn buttons that keep the drawer from pulling out too far; see Fig. 30. Mount them to the bottom side of the middle shelf.

DRAWER GUIDES. To make the drawer guides, rip eight ³/₄"-wide pieces from scrap just thick enough so that each drawer fits when the guides are glued in place. These guides also act as drawer front stops; see Fig. 33.

HANGERS. Finally, to hang the cupboard, drill holes on the back and mount hangers over the holes; see Fig. 31.

FINISH. To finish the cupboard, I used Minwax Puritan Pine Finish and topped it with two coats of tung oil. ∎

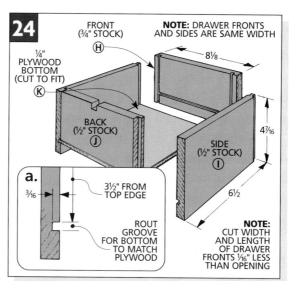

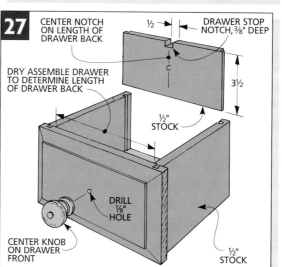

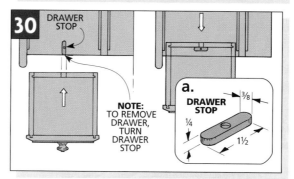

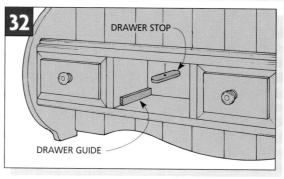

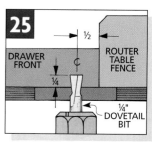

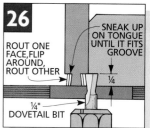

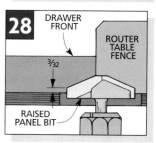

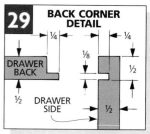

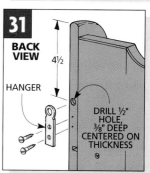

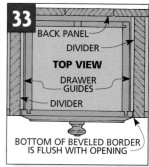

JOINERY . . . . *Tongue & Dado*

It's one of the most frequently used joints in woodworking, and nobody knows what to call it. The joint I'm referring to is a tongue and groove, or a tongue and dado, or a stub tenon and dado. The name changes depending on how it's cut on the workpieces.

For example, it's called a tongue and groove joint when it's used to join two boards edge to edge.

But when this same joint is used to join a shelf to the side of a cabinet, the names change. The groove is now a dado because it's cut across the grain. The tongue might be called a tenon because it's cut on the end rather than the edge.

APPLICATIONS

No matter what you call it, this joint is very handy in cabinet work. Most frequently it's used to join shelves to cabinet sides, or to join the sides to the top and bottom. It can also be used to construct drawers.

In all of these applications, what you're doing is cutting a tongue (or a tenon) to fit in a dado.

But why use this joint in the first place? If you're joining shelves to the sides of a cabinet, why not save time and cut the dado to width to match the thickness of the shelves; see "Full Through Dado" photo above. This way you wouldn't have the extra step of cutting a tongue to fit the dado.

APPEARANCE. The problem is that there can be slight variations in thickness across the width of a shelf, or it's warped slightly. Then the dado is cut to fit the thickest part of the shelf, or it's

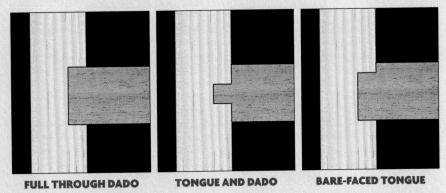

FULL THROUGH DADO   **TONGUE AND DADO**   **BARE-FACED TONGUE**

cut a little too wide to accommodate the warp. So when the joint is assembled, there are gaps.

To produce a cleaner joint, I often cut the dado thinner than the thickness of the shelf; see "Tongue and Dado" photo. Any variations are then hidden inside the joint.

STOPPED DADOES. Another way to improve the appearance of the joint is to cut *stopped* dadoes. If the dado is run all the way across the cabinet side, you will see the joint on the front edge of the cabinet, However, if the dado is stopped 1/2" or so from the front edge, it has a cleaner appearance because the joint isn't exposed.

BARE-FACED TONGUE. There's one more variation on this joint. If the shelf is going to be subjected to considerable weight, the tongue can be made thicker for greater strength.

In this case, the dado is cut only 1/8" narrower than the thickness of the shelf. Then a *bare-faced* tongue is cut on the end of the shelf. (A "Bare-Faced Tongue" is one that has only one shoulder; see photo above.)

Just to add to the confusion, this variation is also called a rabbet/dado joint.

This joint is commonly used to join the top and bottom of a cabinet to the sides, and also to join the back of a drawer to the sides. (See example on opposite page, Fig. 29.) In both of these cases, the rabbet is cut a little deeper to produce a thinner tongue.

CUT THE DADOES

Once the basic configuration of the joint is determined, the next decision to make is which part to cut first, the tongue or the dado.

I've found it's easier to sneak up on the size of the tongue (it's exposed and easier to get to) than it is to adjust the width of the dado. So, I start with the dado, and then cut the tongue to fit.

STOPPED DADO. There are a lot of ways to go about cutting a dado, but the trick is how to cut stopped dadoes on *both* cabinet sides, and make sure they line up exactly. To do this, I use a router and the following procedure.

First, I clamp the two cabinet sides together — back edge to back edge; see Fig. 1. Then mating dadoes can be cut in both pieces at the same time by routing one pass across the boards.

POSITIONING FENCE. The critical part of this procedure is positioning the fence to guide the router. I work off the centerline of the dado. For example, on the wall cupboard the top dado is centered 7 3/4" down from the top edge.

To position the fence, one method is to mark off a distance equal to one-half the diameter of the router's base. If a router with a 6"-dia. base is used, the fence is positioned 3" from the center line of the dado.

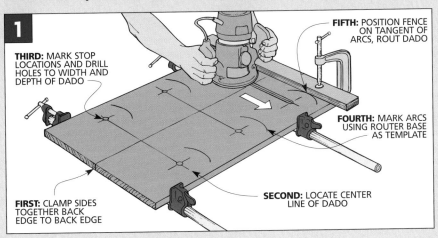

1

THIRD: MARK STOP LOCATIONS AND DRILL HOLES TO WIDTH AND DEPTH OF DADO

FIFTH: POSITION FENCE ON TANGENT OF ARCS, ROUT DADO

FOURTH: MARK ARCS USING ROUTER BASE AS TEMPLATE

SECOND: LOCATE CENTER LINE OF DADO

FIRST: CLAMP SIDES TOGETHER BACK EDGE TO BACK EDGE

PROBLEMS. This method usually works fine, but I've noticed at times the dado has been as much as 1/16" off where it should be.

The problem is that the collet that holds the bit is supposed to be centered on the plastic base. But this is rarely the case. If it's not centered, the distance from the edge of the base to the bit can vary. This means the position of the groove depends on which "edge" of the router base you hold against the fence.

ANOTHER METHOD. After getting frustrated with this approach, I came up with a more accurate procedure.

Clamp the boards edge to edge as before, and mark the points where the dado must stop from the front edge of the cabinet's side piece; see Fig. 1.

At these points, drill a stop hole the same diameter as the width of the dado. (On the wall cupboard, I drilled a 1/4"-dia. hole, 3/8" deep.)

Now here's the trick. Mount a 1/4" straight bit in the router and position the bit *in* one of the stop holes. Then hold the router in the same position it will be during routing and mark a partial arc to indicate the circumference of the base; see Fig. 1. Do the same at the other stop hole.

Then, using these two arcs, align the fence and clamp it in place. To rout the dado, place the router bit in one of the stop holes and rout to the other hole.

Shop Note: Always move the router counterclockwise. Since the guide fence is a straight line, think of "turning the corner" at the end of the fence so the router is moving around the fence in a counterclockwise rotation.

CUT THE TONGUES

After the dadoes are routed in the cabinet's sides, the tongues can be cut on the ends of the shelves. There are actually two problems here.

The tongues have to be cut so they fit snugly in the dadoes. But since tongues are cut on *both* ends of the shelf, the other critical measurement is the distance between the shoulder of the tongue on one end and the shoulder on the other end.

To end up with the correct shoulder-to-shoulder length, cut the shelf to length allowing for the length of the tongues on each end. Then, as the tongues are cut to fit the dado, also be sure to check the shoulder-to-shoulder distance between the tongues.

ROUTER TABLE. If I'm working with shelves made of plywood, I use a router table to cut the tongues. (Plywood seems to chip out less when cut with a router than with a saw blade.)

To set up for the cut, I use a straight router bit that's larger in diameter than the length of the tongue. That is, if the tongue is 1/4" long, I use a 1/2" or 3/4" straight bit on the router table.

Then it's just a matter of adjusting the fence for the length of tongue you want, and raising the bit to cut a rabbet on each face of the shelf. (It's usually best to raise the bit in increments, sneaking up on the thickness of the tongue until it fits snugly in the dado.)

DADO BLADE METHOD. If the shelf is solid wood (rather than plywood), I usually cut the tongue on a table saw or radial arm saw using a dado blade.

TABLE SAW. To use the dado blade on the table saw, attach an auxiliary wooden fence to the table saw's metal fence. Then move the wooden fence over the dado blade; see Fig. 2. Turn on the motor and raise the blade into the fence to cut a relief.

Then turn off the motor and adjust the blade height to cut rabbets on both faces to produce the tongues.

RADIAL ARM SAW. On the radial arm saw, the process is very similar. Just clamp a stop block to the fence and adjust its position so the dado blade will cut a tongue to the exact length needed; see Fig. 3.

TRIM THE TONGUES

As mentioned above, I usually cut stopped dadoes in the cabinet side. This means the front corner of the tongue has to be trimmed to fit the dado.

It's tempting here to use a hand saw to cut down the shoulders and form a notch. But a saw (even a fine dovetail saw) makes a ragged cut. I prefer to use a chisel to get a nice smooth shoulder.

MARK SHOULDER. First I mark the shoulder on the tongue by holding the back of a chisel against one rabbet and roll it halfway over the top of the tongue; see Fig. 4. Then position it on the other rabbet and roll the other side.

When the top has been marked, hold the chisel in this mark and press down firmly to mark the shoulder line. Don't use a mallet yet. It's better to use hand pressure to carefully mark the shoulder line and carve out a small notch.

This small notch sets the shoulder line as it will be seen on the front of the shelf. Once this line is set, it's just a matter of using the chisel and a mallet to chip away a larger notch to fit the stopped dado; see Fig. 4a.

SIZE OF NOTCH. One thing about the size of the notch. It doesn't have to be cut so the notch fits snugly against the front of the stopped dado. In fact, it can be cut back an extra 1/8" or 1/4".

All of the alignment should be done off the back edge because it's easier to get to during assembly.

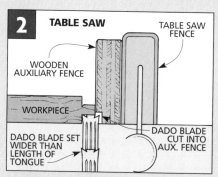

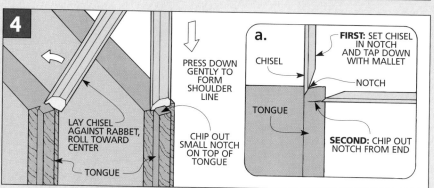

DOVETAILED SHELF

The dovetails on this wall shelf may look like they were cut by hand, but they were actually cut on a band saw.

This wall shelf is a great way to try out the technique of cutting dovetails on a band saw. (For a full explanation of this technique, see pages 34 – 39.) The four sides of the shelf, as well as the drawers, are all joined with dovetails.

A word about dovetails. Dovetails are an age-old joinery technique. Yet, they seem right at home on contemporary furniture, especially those pieces with very simple lines that allow the dovetails to be accented. That's why this shelf is an ideal candidate for dovetails. The joinery provides a nice touch of decoration — and it's a subtle way to show off your craftsmanship.

THE DRAWERS. I also used dovetails to make the three drawers that fit in this shelf. However, with the drawers closed, what you see on the front of the drawer doesn't look like a dovetail — it looks more like a box joint (see photo above). You have to open the drawer to see the characteristic dovetail shape on the drawer's sides.

HANGING SYSTEM. Besides dovetails, this shelf offers another interesting challenge — hanging it on the wall once it's done. Of course, if you use screws or any type of anchor devices, you'll want to drive them into wall studs. Not an easy task. Even if you can locate the studs, there's only a slim chance

they'll be in the right location for hanging the shelf.

Instead, I mounted the shelf by hanging it on a long cleat that is in turn mounted to the wall. The nice part is that the screws can be located anywhere along the length of the cleat. Then the whole system is hidden from view so you don't see any screw heads or even the cleat. (For more on the hanging system; see page 33.)

WOOD AND FINISH. The shelf shown here is made from red oak and finished with two coats of McCloskey's Heirloom Eggshell Varnish. The combination of oak and a matte finish enhances its contemporary look.

EXPLODED VIEW . . . DOVETAILED SHELF

OVERALL DIMENSIONS:
16H x 36L x 8$^{1}/_{16}$D

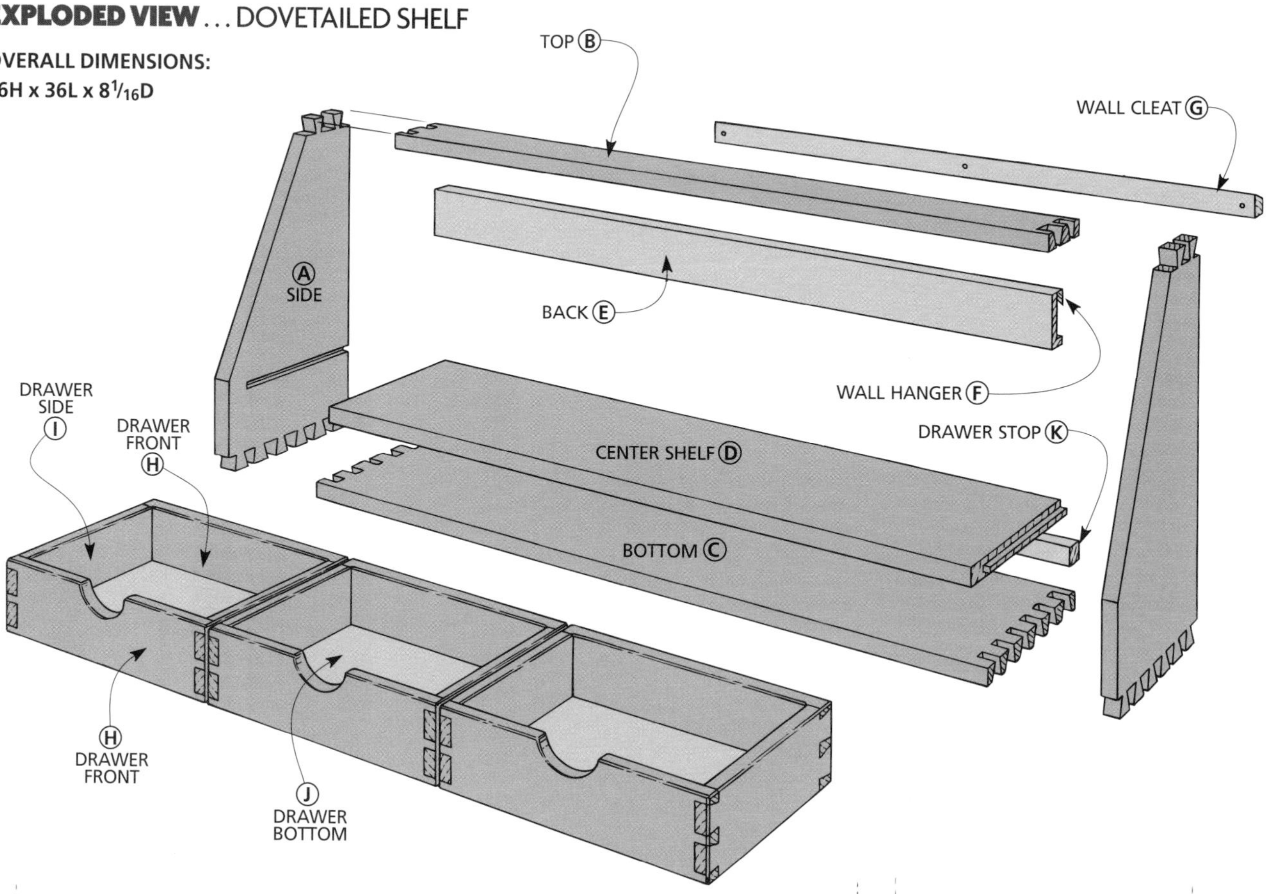

TOP (B)
WALL CLEAT (G)
(A) SIDE
BACK (E)
WALL HANGER (F)
DRAWER STOP (K)
DRAWER SIDE (I)
DRAWER FRONT (H)
CENTER SHELF (D)
BOTTOM (C)
(H) DRAWER FRONT
(J) DRAWER BOTTOM

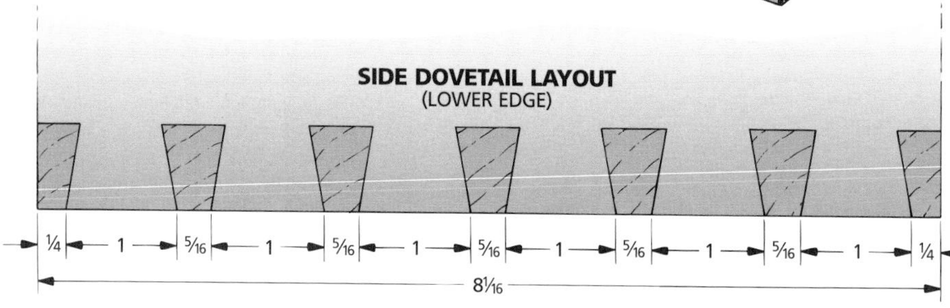

SIDE DOVETAIL LAYOUT
(LOWER EDGE)
¼
1
5⁄16
1
5⁄16
1
5⁄16
1
5⁄16
1
5⁄16
1
¼
8¹⁄16

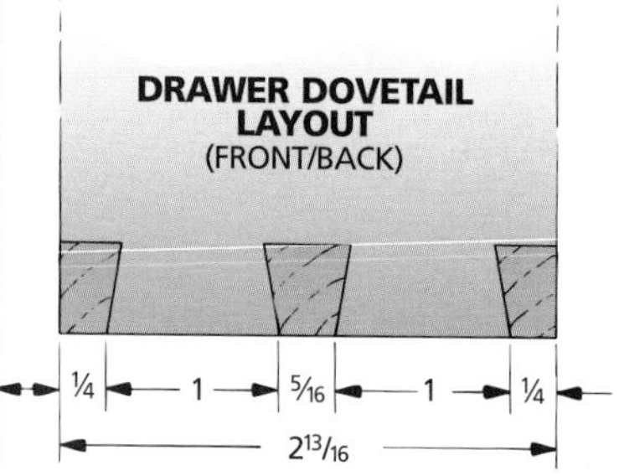

DRAWER DOVETAIL LAYOUT
(FRONT/BACK)
¼
1
5⁄16
1
¼
2¹³⁄16

MATERIALS LIST

SHELF

A	Sides (2)	$^3/_4$ x 8$^1/_{16}$ - 16
B	Top (1)	$^3/_4$ x 2$^{13}/_{16}$ - 36
C	Bottom (1)	$^3/_4$ x 8$^1/_{16}$ - 36
D	Center Shelf (1)	$^3/_4$ x 8$^1/_{16}$ - 35
E	Back (1)	$^3/_4$ x 2$^1/_4$ - 34$^1/_2$

HANGER

F	Wall Hanger (1)	$^1/_2$ x $^3/_4$ - 34$^1/_2$
G	Wall Cleat (1)	$^1/_2$ x 1$^1/_8$ - 34$^1/_2$

DRAWERS

H	Fronts/Backs (6)	$^1/_2$ x 2$^{13}/_{16}$ - 11$^7/_{16}$
I	Sides (6)	$^1/_2$ x 2$^{13}/_{16}$ - 7$^3/_8$
J	Bottoms (3)	$^1/_4$ ply x 7$^1/_8$ - 11$^3/_{16}$
K	Drawer Stop (1)	$^3/_4$ x $^9/_{16}$ - 34$^1/_2$

CUTTING DIAGRAM

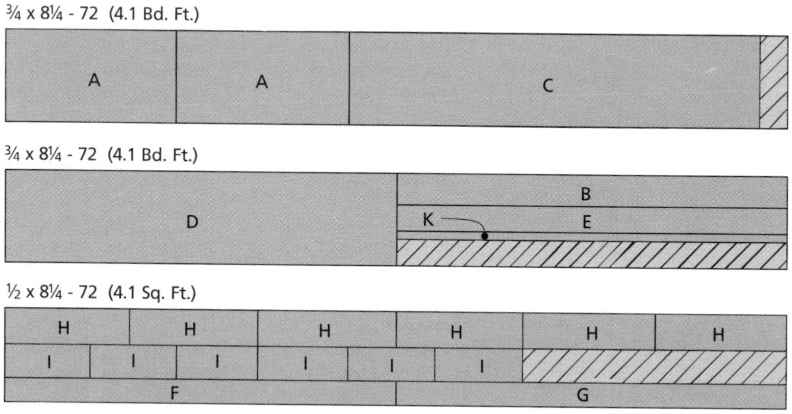

¾ x 8¼ - 72 (4.1 Bd. Ft.)
A
A
C
¾ x 8¼ - 72 (4.1 Bd. Ft.)
D
B
K
E
½ x 8¼ - 72 (4.1 Sq. Ft.)
H
H
H
H
H
H
I
I
I
I
I
I
F
G

Note: Drawers require 12" x 24" piece of $^1/_4$" plywood.

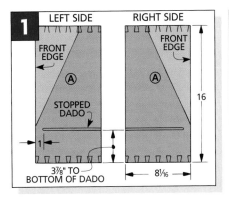

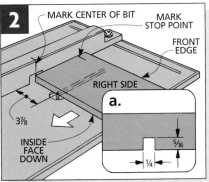

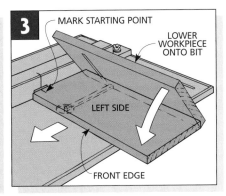

SIDES

I started building the wall shelf by making the two sides (A). Cut these pieces $8\frac{1}{16}$" wide (to accommodate the dovetail layout) and to a length of 16"; see Fig. 1. (The angled front edge of these side pieces will be cut off later.) If you don't have flat, wide boards, build up the width by edge gluing some narrower pieces.

STOPPED DADO. Before cutting the dovetail joints, I routed a stopped dado for the center shelf. This dado is stopped about 1" from the front edge of both side pieces so it doesn't show.

There are a couple of ways to cut these stopped dadoes. You could rout them with a hand-held router as discussed on page 27. This time I decided to use the router table.

To do this, mount a $\frac{1}{4}$" straight bit in the router table and set it to cut $\frac{5}{16}$" deep. Position the fence $3\frac{7}{8}$" from the bit; see Fig. 2.

Since this is a blind cut (the bit is under the workpiece and you can't see where it is), I put a reference mark on the router table fence at the center of the bit; see Fig. 2. Then I put another mark on the workpiece 1" from the front edge to indicate the stopping point for the dado; see Fig. 2.

To rout the dado in the side piece for the right side of the shelf, lay the piece down on the router table and push it through the straight bit, stopping when the two reference marks are aligned; see Fig. 2.

However, for the piece on the left side, you have to make a plunge cut. Turn on the router and slowly lower the workpiece onto the

turning bit. You have to lower it so the reference marks align when the piece is flat on the table. Then push the workpiece across the router table moving from right to left; see Fig. 3.

Shop Note: Although you can accomplish the same thing by routing from left to right, I don't often do it. The rotation of the bit can pull the workpiece away from the fence.

TOP, BOTTOM, SHELF

After the dadoes are routed in the side pieces, you can cut the top and bottom pieces to finished size.

CUT TO SIZE. Start by ripping the top (B) to a width of $2\frac{13}{16}$"; see Fig. 4. Then rip the bottom (C) to match the width of the side pieces ($8\frac{1}{16}$"). As for length, cut both pieces to a uniform length of 36".

DOVETAILS. With the pieces cut to size, you can lay out the dovetail joints. I followed the layout on page 30 laying out the tails on the side pieces and the pins on the top and bottom pieces.

To cut the dovetails, I used the band saw technique shown on pages 34 – 39. There's only one small problem. The angle hasn't been cut off the front edge of the side pieces yet; refer to Fig. 1. But I found it easiest to lay out and cut the

tails all the way across the side pieces to prevent confusion. (You don't have to chop them all out. Just chop out the three waste areas on the side pieces that match the pins on the top piece.)

CENTER SHELF. After the dovetail joints are cut, you can begin work on the center shelf (D). Start by cutting the shelf the same width ($8\frac{1}{16}$") as the sides and bottom; see Fig. 4.

To determine the length of the center shelf, dry assemble the top, bottom and sides. Then measure the inside distance between the sides. (In my case, this was $34\frac{1}{2}$".) Then add $\frac{1}{2}$" for $\frac{1}{4}$"-long tongues (to fit the $\frac{5}{16}$"-deep dadoes) on each end of the center shelf and cut the shelf to length (35").

CUT TONGUES. To make the tongues at the ends of the center shelf, I cut rabbets on the top and bottom faces of the shelf with a dado blade; see Fig. 5. Sneak up on the height of the blade until the tongue fits snugly into the dado in the side piece.

TRIM TONGUES. Since the dadoes on the side pieces are stopped, you have to trim the tongues back; see Fig. 6. To do this, score the front edge with a chisel, and then pare back the tongue just like you did when cutting the dovetails (refer to Step 8 on page 37).

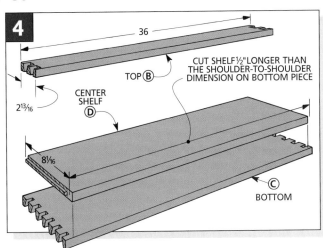

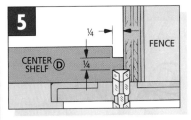

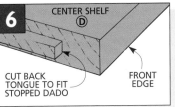

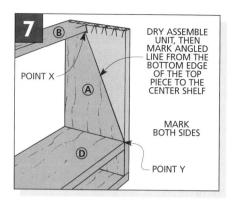

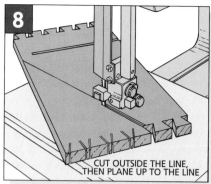

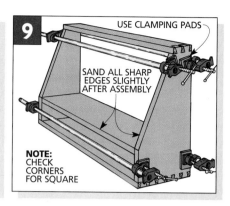

ASSEMBLY

At this point all the joinery is complete. All that remains is to mark and cut the angles off the front of the side pieces.

MARK ENDS. To mark the angles, first dry assemble all of the pieces. Then mark a point "X" where the bottom edge of the top piece (B) meets the side pieces (A); see Fig. 7. Next, mark a point "Y" where the top edge of the center shelf (D) meets the side pieces. Now, disassemble the pieces and draw a line between the marks.

CUT OFF ANGLE. Once the angles are marked, cut just shy of the line with the band saw; see Fig. 8. Then plane to the line with a hand plane.

Now the whole unit can be glued and clamped up; see Fig. 9. (Don't overtighten or the top piece might bow.)

CLEAN UP JOINTS. After the glue dries, check the joints. If the pins and tails stick above the surface of the boards, plane or sand them off flush. If they're slightly recessed, shave the boards down to the pins and tails.

DRAWERS

After building the basic shelf, I built three drawers that would fit the opening between the center shelf and the bottom. The three drawers are simply open boxes with through dovetail corner joints.

CUT THE PIECES. Start building the drawers by cutting the $\frac{1}{2}$"-thick drawer fronts/backs (H) and drawer sides (I) to a width $\frac{1}{16}$" less than the height of the opening. In my case, I cut these pieces $2\frac{13}{16}$" wide; see Fig. 10.

As for length, cut the sides (I) $7\frac{3}{8}$" long. To determine the length of the fronts/backs (H), measure the inside opening on the shelf ($34\frac{1}{2}$") and subtract $\frac{3}{16}$" (to allow space between the drawers). Then, to determine the length of one front/back piece, divide by three ($11\frac{7}{16}$").

DOVETAILS. After cutting the drawer pieces to size, I cut the dovetails following the Drawer Layout shown on page 30. To use the band saw method described on pages 34 – 39, you only need one $1\frac{5}{16}$"-wide spacer block. (Note: The $\frac{1}{2}$" thickness of the drawer parts doesn't effect the basic procedure for cutting the dovetails, just the location of the base lines.)

FINGER HOLE. After cutting the dovetail joints, lay out and cut an offset $1\frac{1}{4}$" radius finger hole on the top edge of each drawer front; see Fig. 11. Then, to make it smooth for fingers, file down the inside edge of the hole; see Fig. 11a.

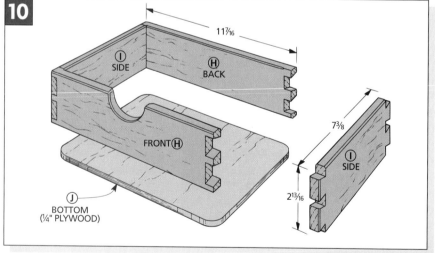

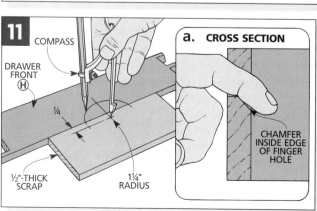

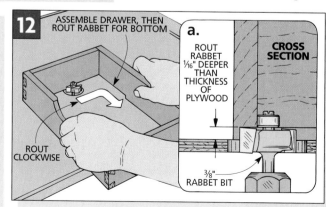

Now glue and assemble the drawers, and check for square.

DRAWER BOTTOM. The drawer bottom (J) fits in a rabbet routed in the bottom edges of the drawer; see Fig. 12a. To do this, mount a $^3/_8$" rabbet bit on the router table and move the assembled drawer around the bit in a clock-wise direction; see Fig. 12. (Note: The rabbet should be slightly deeper than the thickness of the plywood bottom.)

Now cut the drawer bottom from $^1/_4$" plywood , and round the corners to fit in the rabbets; see Fig. 13.

CHAMFER. After gluing the bottoms in place, I softened all the edges of the drawers with a $^1/_{16}$" chamfer; see Fig. 14.

DRAWER STOP. The last step is to add the drawer stop (K); see Fig. 15. It's simply a $^3/_4$" x $^9/_{16}$" strip glued to the shelf bottom at the back of the opening. Position the strip so the drawers stop about $^1/_8$" back from the front edge of the shelf; see Fig. 15a. ∎

13 ROUND CORNERS TO FIT RABBET
BOTTOM (J)
APPLY GLUE TO RABBET LEDGE

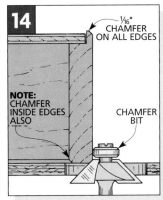

14 $^1/_{16}$" CHAMFER ON ALL EDGES
NOTE: CHAMFER INSIDE EDGES ALSO
CHAMFER BIT

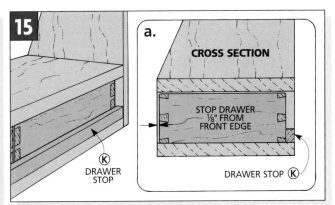

15
DRAWER STOP (K)

a. CROSS SECTION
STOP DRAWER $^1/_8$" FROM FRONT EDGE
DRAWER STOP (K)

Invisible Hanger System

To mount the shelf to the wall, I used a hidden hanging system. It consists of two beveled strips that interlock and permits the mounting screws to be located anywhere (so they can screw into the wall studs, and be hidden).

Start by cutting a shelf back (E) to a rough width of 3" and to length to fit be-tween the shelf sides (A); see Fig. 1.

To accommodate the hidden strips, first cut a $2^1/_2$"-wide groove in the back face of the shelf back (E). I cut the groove by making repeat passes over a dado blade; see Fig. 2.

Then cut this piece $2^1/_4$" wide to produce an L-shaped piece; see Fig. 3.

The shelf actually hangs on two $^1/_2$"-thick inter-locking strips — a hanger and a wall cleat. To make the hanger (F), cut a piece about 2" wide and the same length as the back ($34^1/_2$"). Then bevel-rip off a $^3/_4$"-wide strip; see Fig. 4.

Now follow the same procedure to make the wall cleat (G); see Fig. 5.

Next, glue the hanger (F) to the top back face of the back piece (E). Face the bevel toward the back piece; see Fig. 1a.

Once the glue dries, glue this unit under the top (B) of the wall shelf; see Fig. 1.

Next, screw the cleat (G) to the studs. Then set the shelf over the cleat so the bevels interlock; see Fig. 1a.

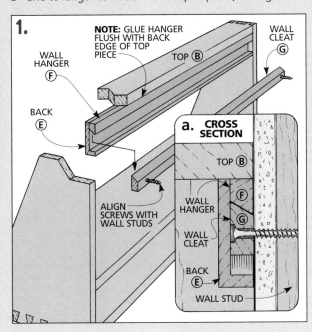

1. NOTE: GLUE HANGER FLUSH WITH BACK EDGE OF TOP PIECE
TOP (B)
WALL CLEAT (G)
WALL HANGER (F)
BACK (E)
ALIGN SCREWS WITH WALL STUDS

a. CROSS SECTION
TOP (B)
WALL HANGER (F)
WALL CLEAT (G)
BACK (E)
WALL STUD

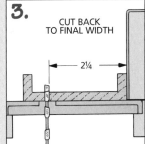

2. BACK (E)
REPEAT PASSES TO CUT GROOVE
3
$2^1/_2$ $^1/_4$
$^3/_4$
$^1/_2$" DEEP

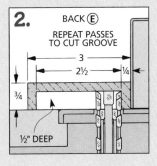

3. CUT BACK TO FINAL WIDTH
$2^1/_4$

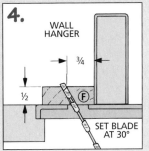

4. WALL HANGER
$^3/_4$
$^1/_2$ (F)
SET BLADE AT 30°

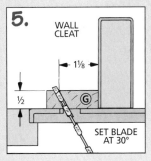

5. WALL CLEAT
$1^1/_8$
$^1/_2$ (G)
SET BLADE AT 30°

When you first take a look at the dovetails on the shelf shown in the photo on page 29, you might think they were cut by hand — or maybe with an expensive router jig. Both the pins and tails of the joint are exposed. (It's actually called a *through* dovetail joint.) But you don't need an expensive jig or a steady hand to cut it.

I cut the through dovetails with a band saw and two shop-built jigs — one to hold the board to cut the tails and one to cut the pins. (These are the two interconnecting parts of a dovetail; see drawing below.)

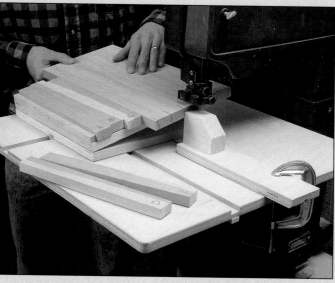

SPACER BLOCK SYSTEM

The basis of the system is a series of spacer blocks. When cutting on the band saw, the blocks space the tail and pin cuts so the two pieces will interlock perfectly. To vary the width of the pins or tails, all you have to do is vary the width of the blocks. Using this system you can create an infinite variety of patterns.

CLEAN INITIAL CUTS. The system solves what I consider to be the most difficult part of cutting through dovetails with hand tools — the initial cuts. They have to be straight, square, and a consistent depth.

LAYOUT TIME. There's another advantage to this system. You don't have to spend a lot of time accurately laying out each joint. I usually lay out the first joint so I don't get confused. But then all the other joints can be cut using the same procedure and they will all be exactly the same.

WIDTH LIMITATION. As with any dovetailing system, there are limitations to this method. The most obvious has to do with the maximum width of the workpieces. Since some of the cutting is done with the workpiece between the blade and the arm of the band saw, the pieces can't be too wide. On my 12" band saw, I found that the workpieces couldn't be much wider than 11½".

PREPARATION TIME. Another disadvantage is the time it takes to build the necessary jigs. If you only want to cut dovetail joints for *one* project, this

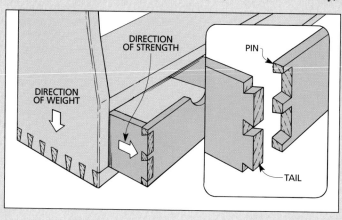

DIRECTION OF STRENGTH

DIRECTION OF WEIGHT

PIN

TAIL

system may not be worth it. You will have to spend a couple of hours building jigs before you can get started cutting joints. But if you expect to cut dovetails in the future, I think the time it takes to build the jigs is well spent.

And, though this system is accurate and flexible, it's not the fastest way to cut dovetails. Even after building the jigs, there's some set-up time and handwork. The band saw doesn't do it all.

HANDWORK. But that's what I like most about this system. I find the handwork that comes with chopping out a dovetail joint especially satisfying. This

band saw system eliminates the hard part — cutting to a line — and allows me to concentrate on the final fit of the joint.

TAILS AND PINS

A through dovetail joint consists of two halves: the tails and the pins. At first it can be a little confusing what is what.

The *tails* look like a dove's tail when viewed from the side of a drawer. The *pins* look like rectangles (sort of like a box joint) when viewed from the front or back of the drawer.

To add to the confusion, when viewed from the ends of the boards, the tails look like pins (usually tall ones), and the pins look like little tails. This all may sound confusing now, but it will clear up once you've cut a few joints.

Okay, which board gets the tails, and which one gets the pins? And does it make a difference? A dovetail joint is *mechanically* strong in only one direction.

On a drawer the pins should be cut on the drawer front; see the drawing at left. Then the mechanical strength of the joint holds the drawer together as it's pulled open. On the shelf (on page 29) the pins are cut on the top to hold up the weight of the whole cabinet, and the bottom to help support the drawers.

LAYOUT

Laying out a dovetail joint — the size and placement of the tails and pins — is worth some time and thought. If the layout isn't on the plan, it's best to draw it out on paper. Then, it can be transferred to the workpieces.

WIDTH OF PIN VS. TAIL. It's a matter of individual preference, but I prefer the pins to be narrower than the tails. Generally, I like the widest part of the tails to be about four times as wide as the narrowest part of the pins.

ANGLES. The angles of the dovetails is also a matter of personal (visual) preference within limits. The general rule is that the angle should be somewhere between 1:5 (78½°) and 1:8 (83°).

When setting up to cut dovetails on the band saw, I found it easiest to build the jigs at an 80° angle. This works out to a ratio of about 1:5¾.

SYMMETRICAL LAYOUT. There's one more thing to consider. When using this technique, the layout has to be symmetrical. That is, one half of the layout has to be a mirrored image of the other half. As long as the layout is symmetrical, you can still vary the width of the tails.

READY TO CUT. After you've decided on the layout, you can transfer it to one end of the board that will have the tails (see the next page). Then you're ready to start cutting your first dovetail joint. (Well, almost. You still have to make the jigs. The first one is explained below.)

(Note: Thanks to Mark Duginske for sharing this dovetail technique with me.)

Auxiliary Band Saw Table

You can cut dovetails on your band saw with only two jigs — the tail jig (shown on page 36) and the pin jig (shown on page 38). But I found it difficult to balance these jigs and a long workpiece on my band saw table.

To solve this problem, I built a 24" x 24" auxiliary table from a piece of ¾" plywood; see Fig. 1. It sits directly on top of the band saw table; refer to Fig. 4.

ADD RUNNER. To hold the auxiliary table in position on the band saw, I glued a ¼"-thick hardwood runner to the bottom of the plywood; see Fig. 1. Cut the runner to width to match the miter gauge slot on your band saw. Then glue it in position so the edge of the auxiliary table clears the arm on the band saw.

NEW SLOTS. After the runner was attached, I cut a slot in the auxiliary table directly over the runner; see Fig. 1a. This slot (dado) is used to guide a runner that's on the bottom of the tail jig. Since I wanted to use my miter gauge for other jobs, I cut it the same size as the slot in my band saw table.

Next, to hold and guide the pin jig, I cut a second slot the same size and at right angles to the first slot; see Fig. 1.

BLADE SLOT. With the slots cut, set the auxiliary table on the band saw and push it into the blade until an 11"-long slot is cut in the plywood; see Fig. 1.

Then, to provide enough of an opening for a stop block, I widened the blade slot to ¼". (Since the runner was attached, I turned the plywood upside down and cut this on the table saw.)

STOP BLOCK. The stop block stops jigs and workpieces that ride on the auxiliary table.

To make the stop, glue a 2½" x 3" block of 1½" stock to the top of a piece of plywood; see Figs. 1 and 2. Glue the block at one end of the plywood, and then cut the ends of the block and plywood off flush. (I also chamfered the bottom edge as a sawdust relief.)

To keep the stop block square on the table, glue a ¼" hardboard runner into a groove cut in the bottom of the stop block; see Fig. 2. The runner slides in the blade slot on the auxiliary table.

TURN BUTTONS. The auxiliary table is held down to the band saw table with a couple of turn buttons. To make the turn buttons, first cut spacer blocks just a hair thinner than the thickness of the band saw table; see Fig. 3.

Next, drill a counterbored hole in the spacer block to accept a carriage bolt. Now insert the bolt into the hole, and then screw the spacer block to the bottom of the plywood table; see Fig. 3. The carriage bolt head should be captured in the counterbore between the block and the plywood.

The turn buttons are rectangular pieces of ¾" plywood with a 5⁄16" hole drilled off center, see Fig. 1. To tighten the turn buttons, you can use a wing nut or a plastic knob.

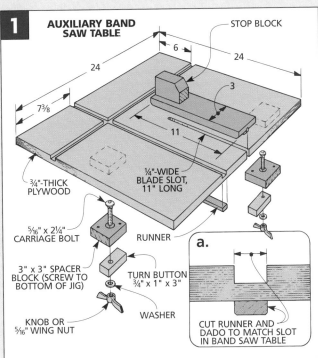

1 AUXILIARY BAND SAW TABLE
STOP BLOCK
6
24
24
7⅜
3
11
¾"-THICK PLYWOOD
¼"-WIDE BLADE SLOT, 11" LONG
5⁄16" x 2¼" CARRIAGE BOLT
RUNNER
3" x 3" SPACER BLOCK (SCREW TO BOTTOM OF JIG)
TURN BUTTON ¾" x 1" x 3"
KNOB OR 5⁄16" WING NUT
WASHER

a. CUT RUNNER AND DADO TO MATCH SLOT IN BAND SAW TABLE

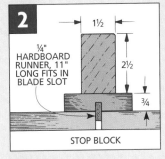

2 1½
¼" HARDBOARD RUNNER, 11" LONG FITS IN BLADE SLOT
2½
¾
STOP BLOCK

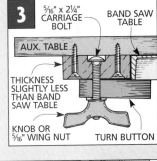

3 5⁄16" x 2¼" CARRIAGE BOLT
BAND SAW TABLE
AUX. TABLE
THICKNESS SLIGHTLY LESS THAN BAND SAW TABLE
KNOB OR 5⁄16" WING NUT
TURN BUTTON

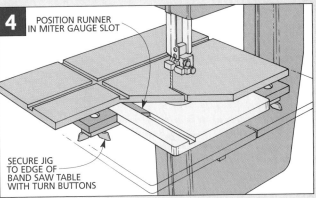

4 POSITION RUNNER IN MITER GAUGE SLOT
SECURE JIG TO EDGE OF BAND SAW TABLE WITH TURN BUTTONS

Cutting the Tails . . . . *Step-by-Step*

Before you begin bandsawing dovetails, there are a few things to do. The band saw has to be tuned up, a tail jig built, and the workpieces prepared.

BAND SAW TUNE UP

To begin, you should spend a few minutes checking that your band saw is tuned up.

BLADE. To cut dovetails, I use a ¼" blade with six teeth per inch. The blade should be sharp and tensioned correctly.

BLADE GUIDES. The most important thing to check is the location of the blade (side) guides — both above and below the table. These hold the blade in line for a straight cut and should be a hair away from the blade.

TAIL JIG

Now you can begin building the tail jig. This jig holds the workpiece at the correct position while cutting.

BASE. Start by cutting a ¾" plywood base 15" wide and 24" long; see Fig. 1.

RUNNER. Next, cut a runner to fit in the miter gauge slot in the plywood auxiliary table; see Fig. 1a. Position the runner on the bottom of the base so the base clears the band saw arm when the runner is in the miter gauge slot.

FRONT FENCE. After the runner is glued in a dado, I screwed a fence on top of the base to hold the workpiece at a 10° angle to the blade. To position the fence, I used my table saw's miter gauge; see Fig. 2.

STOP FENCE. The last part to make is a stop fence. It's a piece of ¾" stock with a squared-off hole cut in it for a C-clamp; see Fig. 3.

STOCK PREPARATION

It's important that any stock to be joined with bandsawn dovetails is flat and planed to a uniform thickness.

SQUARE UP ENDS. After the boards are flat, next square up the ends of the workpieces and cut them to finished size. Then mark the base lines to correspond to the thickness of the matching board; see Step 1 on the opposite page.

CUTTING PROCEDURE

The procedure for cutting the tails is shown on the opposite page. Before you cut dovetails on a project, I'd recommend first working through the whole process — tails and pins — on scrap.

LAYOUT. I start by laying out all the tails; see Step 2. (This isn't really necessary when using spacer blocks, but there's security in seeing the cuts being made where they're supposed to be.)

SPACER BLOCKS. Next, cut spacer blocks from ¾" stock that match the distances from the corner of one tail to the same corner on the next tail; see Step 3. (There will always be one more tail than the number of spacer blocks.) To help keep things straight, I alphabetize the spacer blocks.

STOP FENCE AND BLOCK. Then position the workpiece on the tail jig and clamp down the stop fence; see Steps 4 and 5. Next, push the jig into the blade until the blade touches the base line and clamp down the stop block; see Step 6.

CUTTING. Now it's a matter of adding the spacer blocks one at a time and making cuts; see Cutting Sequence at far right. Then flip the board over and make the second sequence of cuts.

Shop Note: Usually you will be joining both ends of a board with dovetails. To simplify the explanation, I'm showing only one end. Once you're familiar with the sequence, you can flip the board end-for-end and edge-for-edge before adding each spacer block.

CLEAN OUT WASTE. After both sides of the tails are cut, chip out the waste between the tails; see Steps 7 and 8.

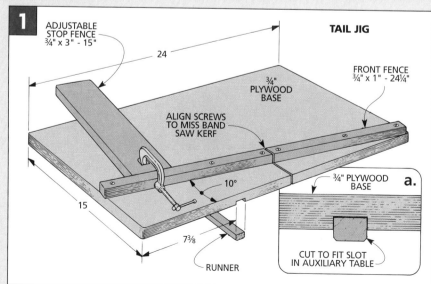

1 ADJUSTABLE STOP FENCE ¾" x 3" - 15"
24
TAIL JIG
¾" PLYWOOD BASE
FRONT FENCE ¾" x 1" - 24¼"
ALIGN SCREWS TO MISS BAND SAW KERF
10°
15
7⅜
RUNNER
a. ¾" PLYWOOD BASE
CUT TO FIT SLOT IN AUXILIARY TABLE

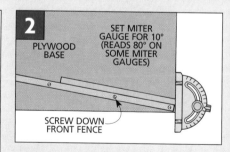

2 PLYWOOD BASE
SET MITER GAUGE FOR 10° (READS 80° ON SOME MITER GAUGES)
SCREW DOWN FRONT FENCE

3 ADJUSTABLE STOP FENCE
1⅝
¾"-DIA. HOLE FOR C-CLAMP HEAD
3
¾
SQUARE UP FRONT EDGE
1

1 Make sure board for tails is true with square ends. Then set the marking gauge to thickness of board for pins. Mark base line on both faces and edges.

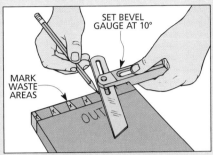

2 For reference when cutting, mark size and spacing of tails on end of the board with a pencil and bevel gauge. Then mark waste areas with an "X."

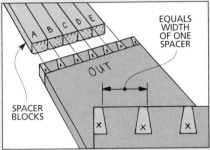

3 To determine the width of each spacer block, measure from upper left corner of one tail to upper left corner of the next tail. Then cut the blocks to size.

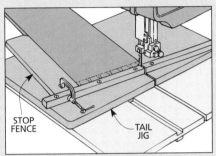

4 Now mount the tail jig on the band saw. Next, set workpiece on the jig and align the first tail with the blade (see Step 5). Then clamp down the stop fence.

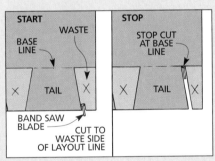

5 For first cut, align blade with line on first tail, left drawing. Then push the jig (and workpiece) into the blade and stop at scribed base line, right drawing.

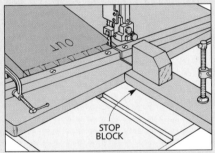

6 Next, clamp the stop block down to the auxiliary table with a C-clamp. Then follow the cutting sequence in box at right. Between cuts, add spacer blocks.

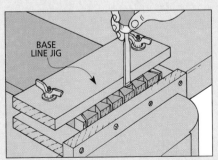

7 To guide the chisel when chopping out the waste, I built a simple jig with a fence. Work from both sides of the board and undercut toward the center.

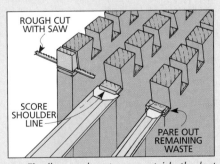

8 Finally, rough cut area outside the last tail 1/16" oversize. Then score the shoulder with a wide chisel (center) and pare out waste with a narrow chisel.

CUTTING SEQUENCE

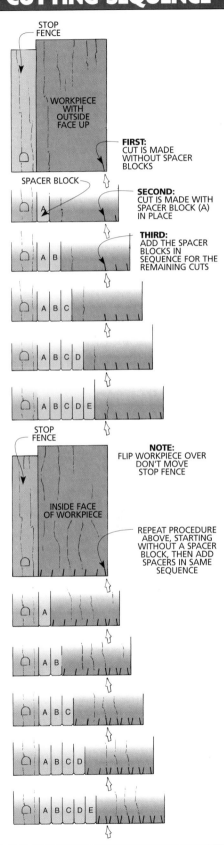

FIRST: CUT IS MADE WITHOUT SPACER BLOCKS

SECOND: CUT IS MADE WITH SPACER BLOCK (A) IN PLACE

THIRD: ADD THE SPACER BLOCKS IN SEQUENCE FOR THE REMAINING CUTS

NOTE: FLIP WORKPIECE OVER DON'T MOVE STOP FENCE

REPEAT PROCEDURE ABOVE, STARTING WITHOUT A SPACER BLOCK, THEN ADD SPACERS IN SAME SEQUENCE

Cutting the Pins . . . . *Step-by-Step*

After you've finished chopping out the waste between the tails, the next step is to cut the pins to fit in those areas. The challenge is getting all of the pins to fit perfectly — not too tight or too loose.

PIN JIG

To cut the pins, there's one last jig to make — the pin jig. It holds the workpiece at an angle to match the tail angle.

CUT TWO SQUARES. The jig is made from two squares of $3/4$" plywood with angled wedges between them; see Fig. 1. I started by cutting the two squares.

RUNNER. Next, cut a 20"-long runner to attach to the bottom of the jig; see Fig. 1. This runner fits in the groove cut across the auxiliary table.

To hold the runner, cut a $1/4$"-deep dado centered on the bottom of one of the plywood squares. Now glue the runner into the dado so an 8"-long tongue sticks out one end; see Fig. 1.

FENCE. After the runner is glued in, the next step is to glue a fence along one edge of the top plywood square; see Fig. 1a. This fence keeps the workpiece and all the spacer blocks in position.

WEDGES. The last pieces to cut are the 12"-long wedges. I cut these off a piece of plywood; see Fig. 2.

Shop Note: To cut a tight-fitting joint, the pin angles must be the same as the tail angles. To make sure they're the same, set the miter gauge off the tail jig; refer back to Fig. 2 on page 36.

ASSEMBLY. Once the wedges are cut, glue them between the two plywood squares to create the angled jig; see Fig. 1.

PIN LAYOUT

After the pin jig is built, you're ready to start laying out and cutting the pins.

Begin by setting the marking gauge to the thickness of the board for the tails and mark base lines on both faces.

MARK CUT LINES. Next, use the tails in the first board to mark the cut lines for the pins on the second board; see Step 1. (Shop Tip: Clamping a small backer board along the base line helps hold the pieces in position.)

Then, to keep everything straight, I mark the waste areas with an "X".

CUTTING PROCEDURE

After the layout is complete, you can mount the pin jig on the band saw; see Step 2. Then align the jig so the blade cuts in the waste area, right next to the line marking that area; see Step 3.

SET STOP BLOCK. Next, set the stop block to keep the cut from going too deep; see Step 4. (Note: The pin jig doesn't move like the tail jig. The workpiece slides forward on the jig.)

MAKE CUTS. Now it's just a matter of making the angled cuts using the same spacer blocks as when cutting the tails.

TURN JIG AROUND. After all of the cuts are made in one direction, turn the jig around and align the blade clearly in the waste area; see Step 5. Then repeat the process of adding spacer blocks and making cuts. After the cuts are complete, chop out the waste between the pins as you did with the tails.

TRIM TO FIT. The most important step is the next one. Check how the pins and tails fit together; see Step 6. Then, if necessary, tap the pin jig over to trim a *little* more off the side of all the pins; see Step 7. (Note: It's easy to take too big of a cut, so just barely move the jig.) Continue sneaking up and cutting until the fit is perfect.

ASSEMBLY

Now comes the fun part. Tap the joint together and check the fit; see Step 8. When the joint fits properly, it can be glued together.

CLEAN UP. Once the joint is together, the pins and tails may stick above the face of the boards, or be recessed. If the end grain sticks above the surface, file the pins or tails flush. If it's recessed, plane the face of the boards down flush with the pins and tails.

1

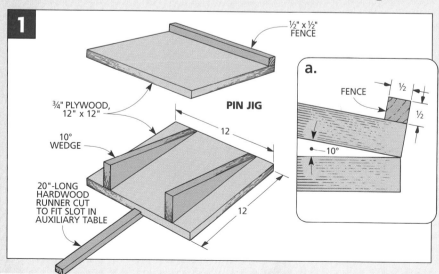

½" x ½" FENCE

PIN JIG

$3/4$" PLYWOOD, 12" x 12"

10° WEDGE

20"-LONG HARDWOOD RUNNER CUT TO FIT SLOT IN AUXILIARY TABLE

12

12

a.

FENCE

½

½

10°

2

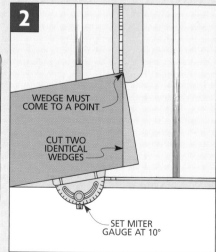

WEDGE MUST COME TO A POINT

CUT TWO IDENTICAL WEDGES

SET MITER GAUGE AT 10°

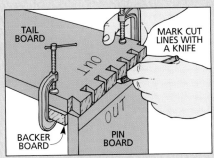

TAIL BOARD — MARK CUT LINES WITH A KNIFE — OUT — OUT — BACKER BOARD — PIN BOARD

1 To lay out pins, first mark base lines on both faces. Then hold tail board on the end of pin board and mark cut lines with a knife. Mark waste areas with "X's"

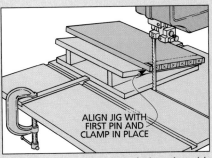

ALIGN JIG WITH FIRST PIN AND CLAMP IN PLACE

2 Mount pin jig and workpiece (outside up) on band saw. Align jig so the blade will cut in waste next to first pin (see Step 3). Then clamp down tongue of jig.

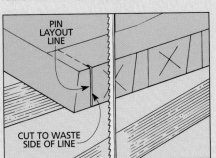

PIN LAYOUT LINE — CUT TO WASTE SIDE OF LINE

3 Note the position of the blade in relation to the layout line. The blade should cut in the waste area so the layout line is just barely "saved."

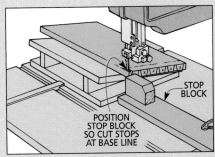

STOP BLOCK — POSITION STOP BLOCK SO CUT STOPS AT BASE LINE

4 Now push workpiece into blade and stop at the base line. Then clamp down the stop block and make cuts shown in cutting sequence at right.

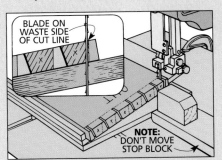

BLADE ON WASTE SIDE OF CUT LINE — NOTE: DON'T MOVE STOP BLOCK

5 Next, turn the pin jig around so angle faces opposite direction. Then align blade alongside the layout line, but clearly in the waste area. Clamp down jig.

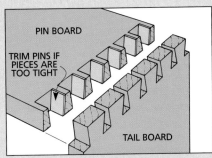

PIN BOARD — TRIM PINS IF PIECES ARE TOO TIGHT — TAIL BOARD

6 After completing cutting sequence, chop out waste areas, then check how pins and tails fit. If they're too tight you can trim a hair more off pins, see Step 7.

ADJUST PIN JIG WITH A LIGHT TAP — OUT

7 To trim off just a hair more, keep the jig clamped to the table and tap the jig with a mallet. You should be able to move it a little without unclamping.

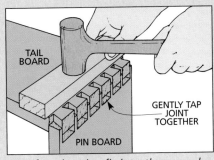

TAIL BOARD — GENTLY TAP JOINT TOGETHER — PIN BOARD

8 After the pins fit into the areas between the tails, the joint can be tapped together. Use a backing board for even pressure and to prevent splitting.

CUTTING SEQUENCE

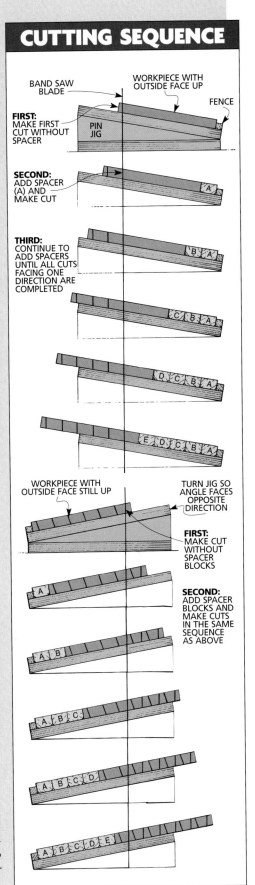

BAND SAW BLADE — WORKPIECE WITH OUTSIDE FACE UP — FENCE

FIRST: MAKE FIRST CUT WITHOUT SPACER — PIN JIG

SECOND: ADD SPACER (A) AND MAKE CUT

THIRD: CONTINUE TO ADD SPACERS UNTIL ALL CUTS FACING ONE DIRECTION ARE COMPLETED

WORKPIECE WITH OUTSIDE FACE STILL UP — TURN JIG SO ANGLE FACES OPPOSITE DIRECTION

FIRST: MAKE CUT WITHOUT SPACER BLOCKS

SECOND: ADD SPACER BLOCKS AND MAKE CUTS IN THE SAME SEQUENCE AS ABOVE

KNOCK-DOWN SHELF

This project is held together without using any permanent joinery or hardware to hold the shelves to the end frames. Yet it's very sturdy.

The primary design feature of this shelf is one you can't see. There's no hardware except fifteen woodscrews. In fact, there's no permanent joinery holding the shelves to the end frames. It all "knocks down" for easy storage or moving.

The shelves rest on dowels in the end frames. This makes the whole unit easy to knock down by just lifting the shelves off the end dowels.

Okay, that makes it easy, but it can't be very sturdy, right? Well, the sturdiness comes from stiffeners that are added to the back edges of the shelves. These stiffeners are cut to fit tight between the end frames to prevent racking (sideways movement). They also serve other purposes. They keep the shelves from bowing under weight,

and they work well as back stops for books so they don't slide off the back edge of the shelf.

MATERIALS. I used ³/₄"-thick red oak to build the shelves and the end frames. And to match these parts, I used oak dowels in the end frames. (If you can't find oak dowels, any hardwood dowels will work.)

SHELVES. One of the first considerations when buying the lumber for a project like this is getting stock that's wide enough for the shelves (9¹/₂" wide). Although that might be the easiest approach, it may not be the best. Wide stock tends to warp easily. Since the shelves in this project are not mounted into dadoes in the end frames, they are particularly susceptible to warp as time goes on.

So, for this project I glued up a couple of narrower strips to make each shelf. The different grain patterns in each strip will help prevent warp. (You will notice in the Cutting Diagram on the opposite page that I have shown two strips for each shelf.)

RADIUS CORNERS. There's one feature on the end frames that's typical on a lot of knock-down furniture projects—a radius is cut on each corner to soften it. To cut these radii, I used a method that produces a uniform radius on every corner. Check out this procedure in the tip box on page 43.

FINISH. This shelf unit is likely to take some abuse, so I finished it with two coats of a durable satin polyurethane varnish, sanding lightly between each of the coats.

CORNER/STIFFENER

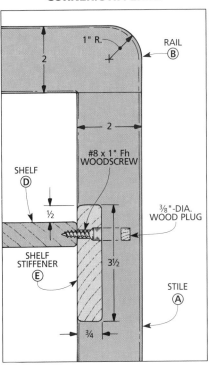

EXPLODED VIEW

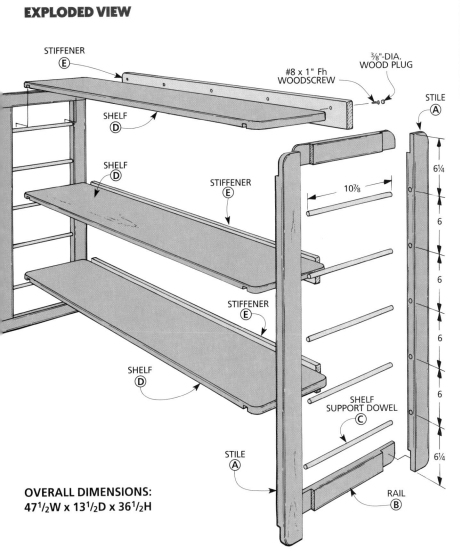

OVERALL DIMENSIONS:
47½"W x 13½"D x 36½"H

SHELF/DOWEL

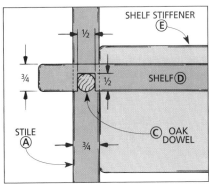

CUTTING DIAGRAM

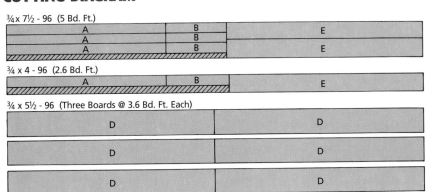

¾ x 7½ - 96 (5 Bd. Ft.)

¾ x 4 - 96 (2.6 Bd. Ft.)

¾ x 5½ - 96 (Three Boards @ 3.6 Bd. Ft. Each)

MATERIALS LIST

WOOD

A	Stiles (4)	¾ x 2 - 36½
B	Rails (4)	¾ x 2 - 13½
C	Sup. Dowels (10)	½ x 10⅞
D	Shelves (3)	¾ x 9⁷⁄₁₆ - 47½
E	Shelf Stiffeners (3)	¾ x 3½ - 44¼

HARDWARE

(15) No. 8 x 1" Fh woodscrews
(15) ⅜"-Dia. wood plugs

STILES AND RAILS

This shelf unit is relatively easy to build — there are only two end frames and three shelves. I started by making the two end frames.

Begin by ripping four stiles (A) and four rails (B) all to a uniform width of 2". Then cut the stiles 36½" long and the rails 13½" long.

END LAPS. After cutting the stiles and rails to size, they're joined with end laps to form the end frames. The end laps are actually wide rabbets on the ends of all the pieces; refer to Fig. 4. The depth of the rabbet equals half the thickness of the piece, and the width should match the mating piece (2").

ROUND OVER EDGES. Before assembling the frame, I rounded over the inside edges of the stiles (A) using a ⅛" roundover bit in the router; see Fig. 1. These edges can't be rounded after the frame is assembled because the dowels will be in the way; refer to Fig. 5.

To keep from routing into the joints on the stiles, I made pencil stop marks 2½" from each end; see Fig. 1.

LAYOUT HOLES. After rounding the edges, I laid out marks to drill a series of holes down the inside edge of the stiles to mount the shelf support dowels.

To get the marks aligned on all four stiles, stack them on edge so the ends are flush, then clamp them together; see Fig. 2. Now mark across the edges, starting 6¼" from an end, then every 6"; refer to the Exploded View on page 41.

CENTER BIT. To center the bit on the thickness of the stile, insert a ½" brad point bit into the chuck, then clamp a 2x4 on the drill press table for a fence; see Fig. 3. Now put the outside face of a stile against the fence. With the drill press off, lower the bit so the bit's point makes a mark in the wood. Flip the stile around, so the other face is against the fence and lower the bit again. If the point on the bit doesn't exactly enter the first mark, adjust the fence and try again until you only make one mark.

DRILL HOLES. Once the bit is centered, drill five holes ¾" deep into the *inside* edge of each stile.

END FRAME ASSEMBLY

After drilling all of the holes for the support dowels, the next steps are to cut the dowels and then assemble the end frame units.

SHELF SUPPORT DOWELS. First, I cut the shelf support dowels (C) to length. To determine the length, measure the distance between the shoulders of the rails (9½"); see Fig. 4. Then add to this measurement the depths of two holes in the stiles. Now cut ten ½"-dia. dowels ⅛" less than this total so they won't bottom out.

INSERT DOWELS. After cutting the dowels to length, insert them between two stiles. (Make sure the lap joints on both of the stiles face the same direction; see Fig. 4.)

ASSEMBLY. To complete the assembly of the end frame, lay the stile assembly flat across two pipe clamps so the end laps face up; see Fig. 5. Next apply glue to the end laps on the rails and clamp them to the end laps on the stiles using three pipe clamps to pull the shoulders tight, as shown in Fig. 5. After the shoulders were tight, I added a C-clamp on each corner to squeeze the end laps together.

RADIUS. Once the glue dried, I cut a 1" radius on all corners, refer to the tip box on the opposite page.

ROUNDOVER. After cutting the radius corners, finish rounding over the inside and outside edges of the end frame; see Fig. 5a.

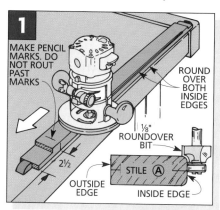

1 MAKE PENCIL MARKS. DO NOT ROUT PAST MARKS. ROUND OVER BOTH INSIDE EDGES. ⅛" ROUNDOVER BIT. OUTSIDE EDGE. STILE (A). INSIDE EDGE. 2½

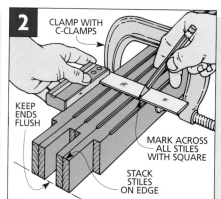

2 CLAMP WITH C-CLAMPS. KEEP ENDS FLUSH. MARK ACROSS ALL STILES WITH SQUARE. STACK STILES ON EDGE.

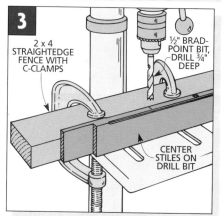

3 2 x 4 STRAIGHTEDGE FENCE WITH C-CLAMPS. ½" BRAD-POINT BIT, DRILL ¾" DEEP. CENTER STILES ON DRILL BIT.

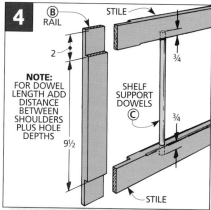

4 (B) RAIL. STILE. 2. NOTE: FOR DOWEL LENGTH ADD DISTANCE BETWEEN SHOULDERS PLUS HOLE DEPTHS. 9½. SHELF SUPPORT DOWELS (C). ¾. ¾. STILE.

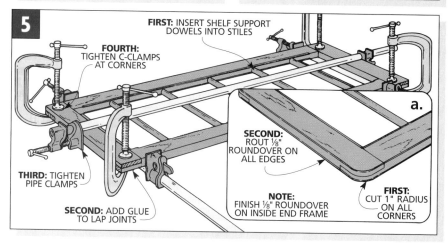

5 FIRST: INSERT SHELF SUPPORT DOWELS INTO STILES. FOURTH: TIGHTEN C-CLAMPS AT CORNERS. THIRD: TIGHTEN PIPE CLAMPS. SECOND: ADD GLUE TO LAP JOINTS. **a.** SECOND: ROUT ⅛" ROUNDOVER ON ALL EDGES. NOTE: FINISH ⅛" ROUNDOVER ON INSIDE END FRAME. FIRST: CUT 1" RADIUS ON ALL CORNERS.

SHELVES

With the end frames finished, work can begin on the three adjustable shelves (D). To prevent the shelves from warping, I edge-glued two boards together to make each shelf blank 11" wide by 48" long.

CUT TO SIZE. After the glue dries, cut the shelves to a finished length of $47^1/_2$". To determine the width, measure the distance between the inside edges of the end frames. Then cut the shelves $1/_{16}$" less to allow for expansion and contraction.

DADOES. After cutting the shelves to width, I cut dadoes on the bottom of each shelf to fit over the shelf support dowels; see Fig. 6. To do this, set the fence $1^1/_8$" from the inside of a $1/_2$"-wide dado blade; see Fig. 6a. Now sneak up on the final depth of the dado by raising the blade and making a pass on a scrap piece until a shelf support dowel fits flush with the bottom of the shelf. Once set, cut dadoes on the bottom face at both ends of all three shelves.

RADIUS AND ROUNDOVER. To complete the shelves, cut a 1" radius on the corners of all the shelves; see tip box above. Then round over all the edges with an $1/_8$" roundover bit.

STIFFENERS

To keep the shelves from bowing and to prevent the whole shelf unit from racking, I added stiffeners (E) to the back edge of each shelf; see Fig. 7.

CUT TO SIZE. Start by ripping enough stock $3^1/_2$" wide to make three stiffeners. To determine the length, assemble the unit, and measure the distance between the end frames along the shelves. Cut the stiffeners to length by

Radius Cutting

One way to round consistent corners is with a template and flush trim router bit. Make the template from hardboard with a 1" radius on one corner. Cut the radius oversize, and *carefully* clean to the line using a disc sander.

To use the template, stick it down on the workpiece using double-sided carpet tape. Cut the radius in several passes, until the bearing rides around the radius of the template.

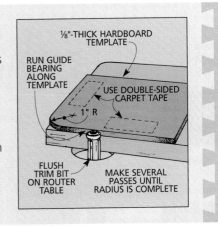

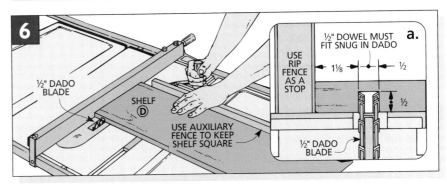

starting a little long, then sneak up on the finished length. Check the fit after each cut until you get a snug fit.

ROUND EDGES. After cutting the stiffeners, round over the edges and ends; see Fig. 7a.

DRILL HOLES. Next, to fasten the stiffeners to the shelves, lay out a series of counterbored shank holes $7/_8$" down from the top edge of each stiffener; see Figs. 7 and 7a for the hole locations. Now drill $3/_8$"-dia. counterbore holes $1/_4$" deep, then $3/_{16}$" shank holes at each of the marks.

FASTEN STIFFENER. After drilling the holes, the stiffener can be screwed to the shelf. I found the easiest way to do this was to lay the front of the unit down flat; see Fig. 7.

To provide a "back lip" for the shelves, position each stiffener so it's $1/_2$" above the top face of the shelf.

Shop Tip: To make sure this height is uniform down the length of the shelf and stiffener, I made a spacer block out of a piece of scrap to use as a gauge. Just cut a $1/_2$" notch out of one corner of the block; see Fig. 8.

When the stiffener is aligned, drill a pilot hole and screw the stiffener down with a No. 8 x 1" Fh woodscrew. After fastening, move the spacer block to the other end of the shelf and repeat the procedure.

PLUGS. With all the screws down tight, I glued wood plugs into the counterbored holes in the stiffeners, and trimmed them off flush; see Fig. 8a. ■

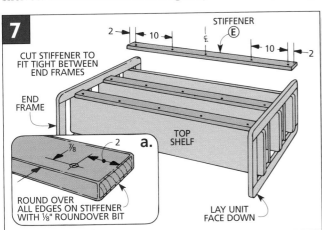

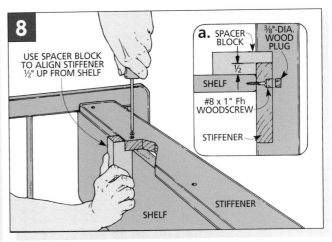

TOWER BOOKCASE

Sometimes smaller is actually better. The narrow design of this bookcase means it will fit into just about any location.

W ho couldn't use a little more storage space around their home? Especially when you don't have to sacrifice a lot of floor space to get it. That's the idea behind the simple design of this tower bookcase.

It takes up less than two square feet of floor space because everything is stored vertically. Yet the six shelves (four of them adjustable) can store or display a variety of items.

One thing unique about the adjustable shelves is how they're held in the case. Dowel pins fit into grooves on the ends of the shelves. So with the shelves installed the dowels are hidden.

But I think the best feature of the tower bookcase is its mobility. The compact size and light weight make it easy to move this bookcase anywhere extra storage space is needed.

JOINERY. Basic tongue and groove joints are all that are needed to hold the case together. And building the top and bottom molding and attaching them to the case is straightforward too.

WOOD. I built the sides and shelves of this bookcase from $3/4"$ cherry plywood (one 4x8 sheet is more than enough) and the back from a half sheet of $1/4"$ cherry plywood. The sides and shelves are all edged with solid cherry. (See the special box with some tips on trimming the edging flush on page 47.)

FINISH. I wanted a deep cherry stain for the this project so I mixed together two parts Bartley's Pennsylvania Cherry Gel Stain with one part Bartley's Restoration Red Gel Stain. Once the stain dried, I topped it off with three coats of General Finishes' Royal Finish.

EXPLODED VIEW

TOP MOLDING
(H)

SIDE VIEW

ADJUSTABLE
SHELF
(I)

FIXED SHELF

(C)

ADJUSTABLE SHELF
EDGING
(J)

CASE SIDE
(A)

SHELF
HOLE
SPACING

FIXED SHELF
(C)

CASE BACKS
(E)

23⅝

11⅝

(D)

FIXED SHELF
EDGING

2

8

CASE EDGING
(B)

¼"-DIA.
HOLES,
⅜" DEEP

1

CLEAT
(F)

BASE
MOLDING
(G)

23⅝

1
1

(C)

11⅝

OVERALL DIMENSIONS:
77⅜H x 20W x 14D

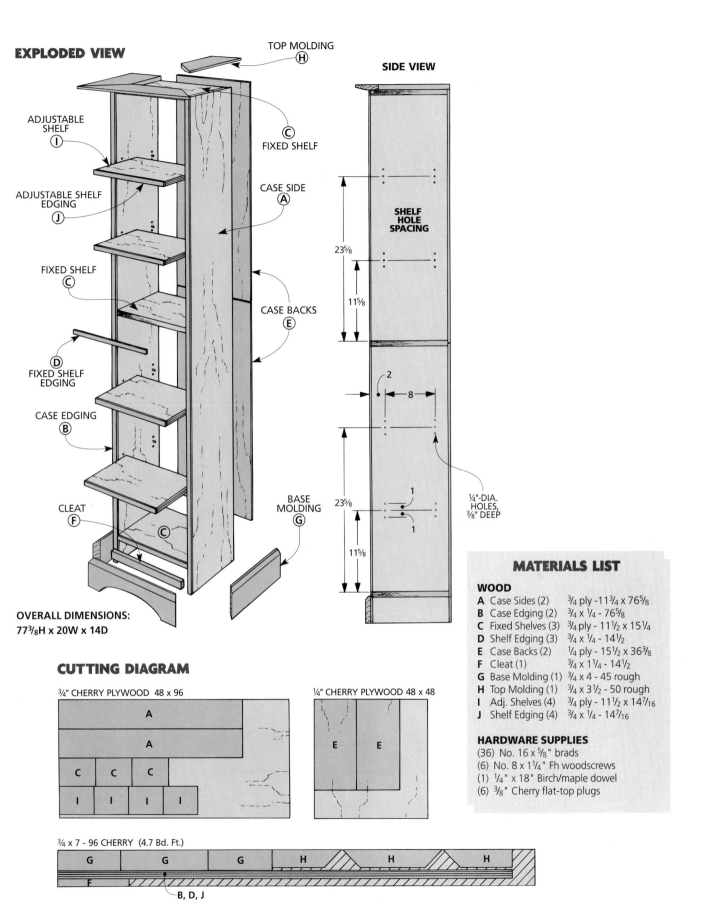

MATERIALS LIST

WOOD
A Case Sides (2)   ¾ ply -11¾ x 76⅝
B Case Edging (2)   ¾ x ¼ - 76⅝
C Fixed Shelves (3)   ¾ ply - 11½ x 15¼
D Shelf Edging (3)   ¾ x ¼ - 14½
E Case Backs (2)   ¼ ply - 15½ x 36⅜
F Cleat (1)   ¾ x 1¼ - 14½
G Base Molding (1)   ¾ x 4 - 45 rough
H Top Molding (1)   ¾ x 3½ - 50 rough
I Adj. Shelves (4)   ¾ ply - 11½ x 14⁷⁄₁₆
J Shelf Edging (4)   ¾ x ¼ - 14⁷⁄₁₆

HARDWARE SUPPLIES
(36) No. 16 x ⅝" brads
(6) No. 8 x 1¼" Fh woodscrews
(1) ¼" x 18" Birch/maple dowel
(6) ⅜" Cherry flat-top plugs

CUTTING DIAGRAM

¾" CHERRY PLYWOOD 48 x 96

A

A

C   C   C

I   I   I   I

¼" CHERRY PLYWOOD 48 x 48

E   E

¾ x 7 - 96 CHERRY (4.7 Bd. Ft.)

G   G   G   H   H   H

F

B, D, J

CASE

The case is the heart of this project. It's just an upright box with three fixed shelves installed between two vertical sides; see Fig. 1.

SIDES. The vertical case sides (A) are cut first to finished size. They're ripped from a sheet of 3/4" plywood.

Shop Note: When cutting the pieces to length, it's a good idea to use a plywood blade or a crosscut blade with at least 50 teeth. It will help reduce the amount of chipout on the ends.

With the sides cut to size, the next step is to cut 1/4"-wide dadoes at both ends and across the middle. Later these dadoes hold the fixed shelves.

To cut the dadoes, I used a 1/4" straight bit in a hand-held router. I was tempted to use a dado blade in the table saw. But the pieces are just too long to handle easily. Especially when you're trying to cut the dadoes near the ends of the sides.

The easiest way to rout the dadoes is to lay the sides edge-to-edge with the inside faces up (like an open book); see Fig. 2. Then rout each set of dadoes in one pass using a straightedge to guide the router.

EDGING PLYWOOD. With all three sets of dadoes cut, the front edge of the plywood sides can now be covered to hide the plies and "stop" the dadoes.

To do this, I ripped two long strips of 1/4"-thick case edging (B) from a piece of 13/16"-thick hardwood stock.

Shop Note: Whenever possible, I'll use edging strips trimmed off the edge of a piece of 13/16"-thick stock. Since that's a little thicker than the 3/4" plywood, alignment with the plywood isn't critical; refer to Fig. 3a. It can be trimmed flush later.

Another tip to make installing the edging a little easier is to use spacers (strips of 1/4"-thick hardboard) under the plywood when gluing; see Fig. 3. They raise the plywood off the clamps so you can keep the edging centered; see Fig. 3a.

The spacers also help create more direct pressure when clamping. Raising the plywood pieces puts them in line with the screw on the clamp.

I also like to use a pressure block between the clamp head and the edging. It helps distribute the clamping pressure, so fewer clamps are needed; see Fig. 3. Plus, it protects the edging

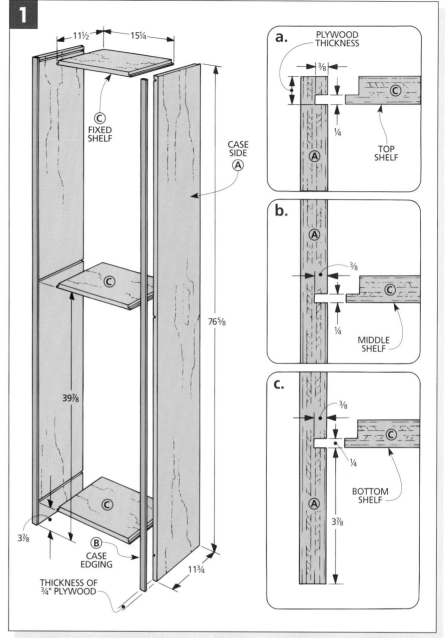

from dents and scratches from the clamp jaw.

TRIM EDGING. After the glue dries, the edging can be trimmed flush. To do

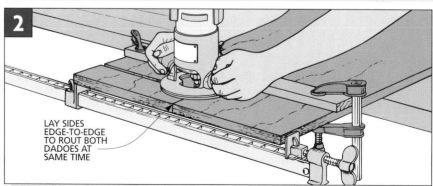

this I used a router with a flush trim bit. For more on this, see the box on page 47.

BACK RABBET. With the edging trimmed on the front edges of the case sides, a rabbet can be cut on the back edges; see Figs. 4 and 4a. This creates a recess for a plywood back that's installed later.

FIXED SHELVES. To join the sides together, three fixed shelves (C) are glued near the top, middle, and bottom of the case; see Fig. 1.

I started by cutting the shelves to finished size from ³/₄" plywood. Next, ¹/₄" tongues are cut on both ends; see Figs. 1a, b, c. These tongues are sized to fit in the dadoes cut in the side pieces.

CASE ASSEMBLY. Once the tongues on the shelves fit snug in the sides, the case can be assembled. To do this, slide in the shelves until the front edges of the tongues butt up against the edging strips at the front of the case. At the same time the shelves should sit flush with the shoulders of the rabbets on the back of the case. (If needed, trim the shelf's back edge until it's flush.)

Finally, glue and clamp the fixed shelves between the side pieces. Check that everything is square after the clamps are tight.

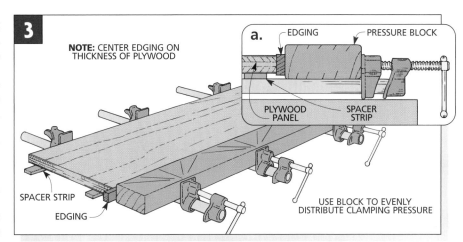

3

NOTE: CENTER EDGING ON THICKNESS OF PLYWOOD

a. EDGING   PRESSURE BLOCK

PLYWOOD PANEL   SPACER STRIP

USE BLOCK TO EVENLY DISTRIBUTE CLAMPING PRESSURE

SPACER STRIP

EDGING

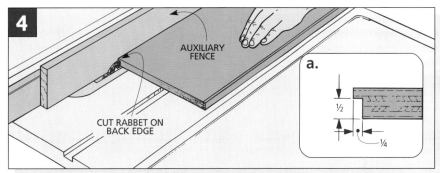

4

AUXILIARY FENCE

a.

½

¼

CUT RABBET ON BACK EDGE

Trimming Edging Flush

Once the edging was glued on the sides of the tower bookcase, it needed to be trimmed flush. To do this, I used a router with a flush trim bit.

To prevent the bearing from dropping in the dadoes in the sides, I filled in each dado with a filler strip that was just thick enough to fit flush with the face of the plywood; see Fig.1

The trick to keeping the router from tipping when working on the thin edges is to clamp both side pieces together. It gives a wider surface for the router to sit on. And it lets you rout the edging on both pieces at the same time.

To make this work, you'll have to separate the case sides to make room for the router bit. I clamped 2x4 spacers between the sides to hold them apart and make a wide platform for the router; see photo at right and Fig. 2.

Finally, I trimmed the edging to length with a sharp chisel; see Fig. 3.

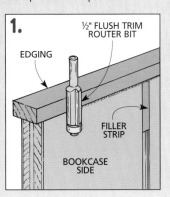

1.

½" FLUSH TRIM ROUTER BIT

EDGING

FILLER STRIP

BOOKCASE SIDE

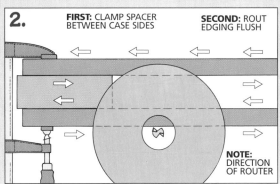

2.

FIRST: CLAMP SPACER BETWEEN CASE SIDES

SECOND: ROUT EDGING FLUSH

NOTE: DIRECTION OF ROUTER

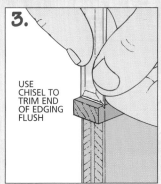

3.

USE CHISEL TO TRIM END OF EDGING FLUSH

EDGING, BACK, AND CLEAT

With the case assembled and glued together, I wanted to hide the plies on the fixed shelves the same way the side pieces were covered. To do that, strips of shelf edging (D) are glued to the top, bottom, and middle fixed shelves; see Fig. 5 and the box below.

BACK. Now is a good time to enclose the back of the case. Normally, it's about the last thing I do. But on a tall narrow project like the bookcase, it's easy to rack the sides just moving it around the shop. Adding back pieces now strengthens the case.

The two case backs (E) are cut from a half sheet of $1/4$"-thick plywood; see Fig. 5. You may wonder why I used two pieces instead of just one. It's economics. By using two pieces, I could cut both from a half sheet of plywood instead of having to buy a full sheet. Note: Don't worry about the "seam" where the two back pieces meet. It'll be hidden behind the middle fixed shelf; see Fig. 5b.

Now install the case backs in the rabbets cut in the case sides. To do that, I used glue and brads.

CLEAT. To complete construction of the case, a cleat (F) is attached to the bottom fixed shelf; see Fig. 5c. This cleat is a $3/4$"-thick piece of stock glued and clamped flush with the front. It's added to create more glue surface for attaching the front piece of base molding (added next).

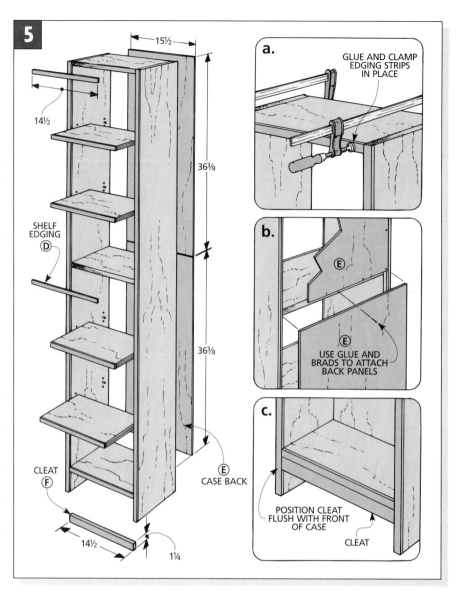

Aligning and Clamping Edging

When it came time to install edging to the fixed shelves on the tower bookcase, I ended up doing things a little differently. Instead of installing oversize pieces that get trimmed flush later, I cut the edging to exact size and glued it in place.

The reason for doing things differently is the narrow edge on the shelf. It's too easy for the router and flush trim bit to tip and gouge the edging. By cutting the edging to an exact fit, only a little light sanding is needed.

One problem you run into when applying edging this way is keeping it aligned with the edge of the plywood. After the glue is applied, the edging seems to want to slide out of place.

My solution to this problem is to use scrap blocks to help align the edging. First, I clamp the scrap blocks to both sides of the shelf. They form a slot for the edging to fit into.

To "clamp" the edging in place, I'll use duct tape to pull it tight against the shelf until the glue dries.

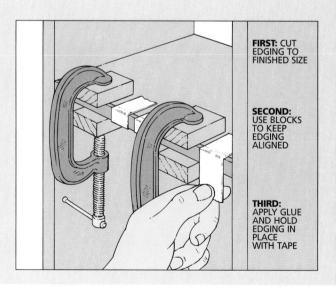

FIRST: CUT EDGING TO FINISHED SIZE

SECOND: USE BLOCKS TO KEEP EDGING ALIGNED

THIRD: APPLY GLUE AND HOLD EDGING IN PLACE WITH TAPE

MOLDING

With the case complete the next step is to add the molding at the top and bottom.

BASE MOLDING. The easiest way to make the base molding (G) is to start with one long board and rip it to finished width; see Fig. 6. Next, rip or rout a 45° chamfer along one edge; see Fig. 6a. Now this long blank can be mitered into three pieces to fit around the base.

Before attaching the base molding to the case, a half ellipse is cut in the front piece to add a decorative detail.

To create this shape, first enlarge the half pattern in Fig. 7. It isn't critical that you match the pattern exactly. But what you want to end up with is a design that looks balanced on the front piece.

The way I went about doing that is to first find the centerline of the front piece. Then position the half pattern on one side of this line and trace around it to draw one half of the partial ellipse; see Fig. 8. Now by flipping the pattern over, the other half of the ellipse can be drawn next. When you're finished, the ellipse will be automatically centered.

Now cut out the shape and use a drum sander to sand the ellipse smooth. Finally, all three pieces can be glued and clamped to the case.

TOP MOLDING. To complete the molding for the case, top molding (H) is added next; see Fig. 9. This is made in much the same way as the base molding. First, a blank for all three pieces is ripped to finished width. Next, a 12° bevel can be ripped on one face; see Fig 9a.

Now miter the ends of the pieces to fit around the top with a 2" overhang. Each piece can be glued and screwed in place to form a U-shaped frame to sit on top of the case. Finally, plug the screw holes to fill in the openings.

SHELVES

Now, all that's left for this bookcase is to add the rest of the shelves. So make four adjustable shelves (I) to fit inside the case; see Fig. 10. These shelves are the same width as the fixed shelves (C) that hold the case together (11 $\frac{1}{2}$"). As for their length, I cut the shelves $\frac{1}{16}$" shorter than the opening in the case.

The only thing unusual about the adjustable shelves is the way they're held in the case. It's a system of shelf support pins that fit in holes in the case. Not too unusual. But the shelves don't rest on top of the support pins. Rather, they fit *around* the pins; see Fig. 10a. It's all done with a simple groove in the ends of the shelves.

To cut the $\frac{1}{4}$"-wide groove, I used a dado blade in the table saw. Note: The grooves should be centered on the thickness so they sit level.

SHELF EDGING. After cutting the grooves on the four adjustable shelves, a piece of shelf edging (J) is glued and clamped to the front edge of each shelf. The edging hides the grooves as well as the plies of the plywood.

DOWEL PINS. To support the shelves in the bookcase and make them adjustable at the same time, short pins cut from $\frac{1}{4}$"-diameter dowel rod are installed in holes drilled in the sides of the case. The location of the $\frac{1}{4}$" holes to accept the pins is shown in the side view on page 45. Note: I drilled three hole positions for each adjustable shelf.

Finally, cut four shelf support pins from the dowel rod for each of the shelves. Because the pins need to be removable, I didn't stain or finish them. Just add a coat of wax so they will be easy to pull out when changing the height of the shelves. ■

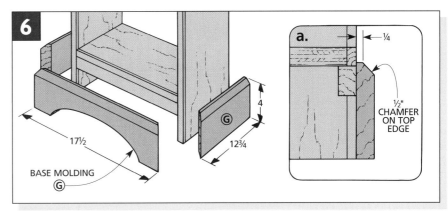

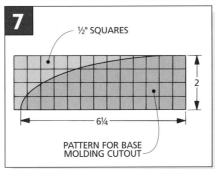

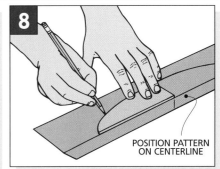

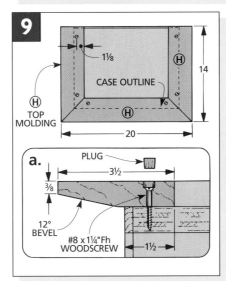

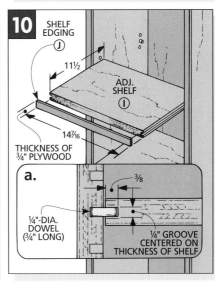

WALL UNIT

This unit only takes two and a half sheets of plywood to build, but the shelves are deep enough to display books and collectibles.

When you set out to build a large project like this wall unit, plywood is an ideal material to work with. It's flat, dimensionally stable, and comes in sheets large enough so you don't have to go through the tedious process of edge-gluing a lot of boards together.

However, there are two main disadvantages to plywood. The edges have to be covered in some way to hide the plies. And, the project has to be designed around the fact that plywood comes in 4 x 8 sheets.

To get the most efficient use of each sheet, I had to juggle the size of all the pieces to fit a certain cutting diagram. I also had to watch the grain direction — especially with the doors. Here I tried to arrange the pieces on the sheet to get the nicest grain pattern on the two doors.

JOINERY. I decided to use tongue and groove joints throughout this project, beginning with the primary joint to join the three fixed shelves to the case sides.

To join these pieces, I cut a $\frac{1}{4}$"-wide dado across the inside face of the sides. Then tongues are cut on the ends of the shelves.

But why cut a $\frac{1}{4}$"-wide dado? Why not make it $\frac{3}{4}$" wide to match the thickness of the plywood?

I used $\frac{3}{4}$" oak plywood, which is rarely exactly $\frac{3}{4}$" thick — it's usually just slightly less. It can also have slight variations in thickness throughout the sheet (usually due to the final sanding each sheet gets). So, rather than take a chance on a sloppy fit, or on a joint line that looks wavy, I cut a $\frac{1}{4}$"-wide dado, and then cut a tongue to fit.

EDGING. In addition to using tongue and groove joinery as the primary joint to assemble the case, I also used it to attach edging strips to hide the edges of the case sides and shelves. Although the edging could be glued on with just a plain butt joint, using a tongue and groove joint helps align the edging. (For more on this, see pages 57–58.)

FINISH. When the case was done, I decided to apply two coats of Minwax golden oak stain. Then I finished it off with two coats of McCloskey's Heirloom semi-gloss varnish.

EXPLODED VIEW

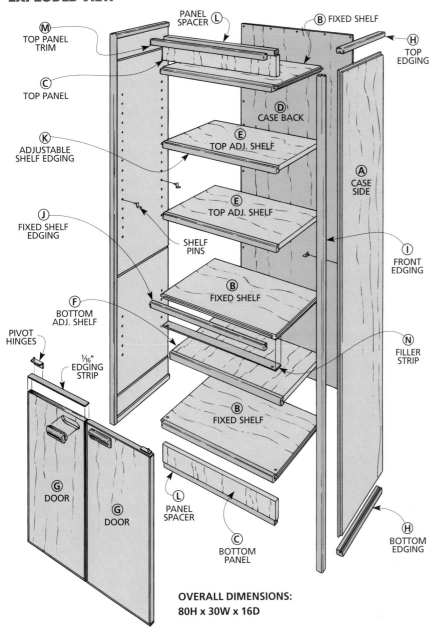

- Ⓜ TOP PANEL TRIM
- Ⓛ PANEL SPACER
- Ⓑ FIXED SHELF
- Ⓗ TOP EDGING
- Ⓒ TOP PANEL
- Ⓓ CASE BACK
- Ⓚ ADJUSTABLE SHELF EDGING
- Ⓔ TOP ADJ. SHELF
- Ⓐ CASE SIDE
- Ⓔ TOP ADJ. SHELF
- Ⓙ FIXED SHELF EDGING
- SHELF PINS
- Ⓑ FIXED SHELF
- Ⓘ FRONT EDGING
- Ⓕ BOTTOM ADJ. SHELF
- PIVOT HINGES
- ¹/₁₆" EDGING STRIP
- Ⓝ FILLER STRIP
- Ⓖ DOOR
- Ⓖ DOOR
- Ⓑ FIXED SHELF
- Ⓛ PANEL SPACER
- Ⓒ BOTTOM PANEL
- Ⓗ BOTTOM EDGING

OVERALL DIMENSIONS:
80H x 30W x 16D

CROSS SECTION

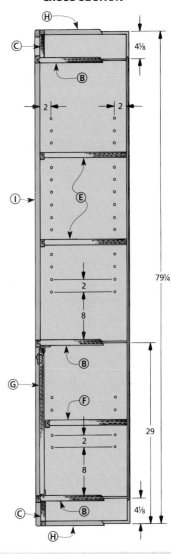

- Ⓗ
- Ⓒ
- 4¹/₈
- Ⓑ
- 2   2
- Ⓘ
- Ⓔ
- 79¹/₄
- 2
- 8
- Ⓑ
- Ⓖ
- Ⓕ
- 29
- 2
- 8
- Ⓒ
- Ⓑ
- 4¹/₈
- Ⓗ

CUTTING DIAGRAM

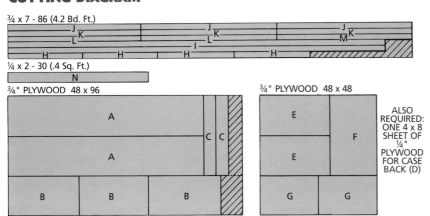

¾ x 7 - 86 (4.2 Bd. Ft.)

¼ x 2 - 30 (.4 Sq. Ft.)

¾" PLYWOOD 48 x 96

¾" PLYWOOD 48 x 48

ALSO REQUIRED: ONE 4 x 8 SHEET OF ¼" PLYWOOD FOR CASE BACK (D)

MATERIALS LIST

WOOD

A	Case Sides (2)	¾ ply - 15⅝ x 79¼
B	Fixed Shelves (3)	¾ ply - 15⅜ x 29¼
C	Top/Btm. Pnl. (2)	¾ ply - 28½ x 3½
D	Case Back (1)	¼ ply - 29½ x 70¾
E	Top Adj. Shelv. (2)	¾ ply - 14⅜ x 28⅜
F	Btm. Adj. Shelf (1)	¾ ply - 28⅜ x 13½
G	Doors (2)	¾ ply - 13¹¹/₁₆ x 23½

SOLID TRIM EDGING

H	Top/Bottom (4)	¾ x 1 - 15¼
I	Front Sides (2)	¾ x 1 - 80
J	Fixed Shelves (3)	¾ x 1 - 28
K	Adj. Shelves (3)	¾ x 1 - 28⅜
L	Panel Spacers (2)	¾ x ¾ - 28
M	Top Panel Trim (1)	¾ x 1 - 28
N	Filler Strip (1)	¼ x 1½ - 28½

HARDWARE SUPPLIES

- (32) No. 6 x ¾" Fh woodscrews
- (12) ¼" Brass shelf supports
- (2) Recessed red oak door pulls
- (2 pr.) Pivot hinges
- (1) Double plate magnetic catch
- (2) Adjustable levelers

CASE SIDES

I started work on this wall unit by making two case sides (A). Although the sides are just two pieces of plywood, they present a problem. Each side has three sets of dadoes for the fixed shelves (B) — and these dadoes have to be perfectly aligned so the shelves lay flat and parallel. The trick is to cut the dadoes across one wide blank of plywood. Then cut the blank in half to get two identical pieces that can be used as the case sides; see Fig. 1.

CUT TO SIZE. To do this, first cut a large blank to a rough width of 32", and a finished length of 79¼"; see Fig. 1. (Remember, this wide blank will be ripped in half later.)

TONGUES. Before the blank is ripped in half, there are two things that have to be done with it. First, tongues are cut on all four edges; see Figs. 1 and 2a. These tongues are used to attach hardwood edging; refer to Fig. 6. (Beginning on page 57, there's information about adding edging to plywood with tongue and groove joints.)

Procedural Note: When I had the router all set up to rout the tongues, I went ahead and routed the same tongues on each of the six shelves (B, E, and F). (See Fig. 3 on the opposite page.)

DADOES FOR SHELVES. Next, I routed three dadoes for the fixed shelves (B) across the large blank; see Figs. 1 and 2b. To do this, mark the location of the three dadoes. Then clamp a fence to the plywood blank and rout each dado. (See box below for a simple gauge to help align the fence.)

CUT CASE SIDES. Now, to get the two case sides (A), I ripped the plywood blank into two pieces, each 15⅝" wide.

BACK PANEL RABBET. The last thing to do is to rout a rabbet on the back edge of each case side to attach the case back (D); see Fig. 2c.

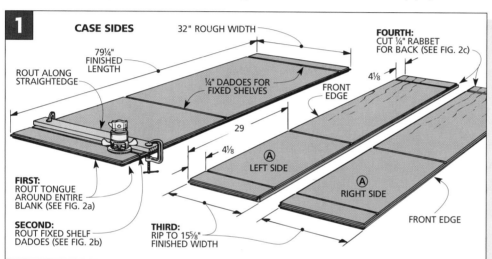

1 CASE SIDES — 32" ROUGH WIDTH — 79¼" FINISHED LENGTH — ROUT ALONG STRAIGHTEDGE — ¼" DADOES FOR FIXED SHELVES — FRONT EDGE — 4⅛ — FOURTH: CUT ¼" RABBET FOR BACK (SEE FIG. 2c) — 29 — 4⅛ — (A) LEFT SIDE — (A) RIGHT SIDE — FRONT EDGE — FIRST: ROUT TONGUE AROUND ENTIRE BLANK (SEE FIG. 2a) — SECOND: ROUT FIXED SHELF DADOES (SEE FIG. 2b) — THIRD: RIP TO 15⅝" FINISHED WIDTH

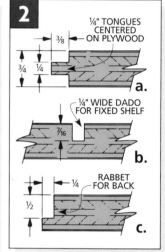

2 — ¼" TONGUES CENTERED ON PLYWOOD — ⅜ — ¾ — ¼ — **a.** — ¼" WIDE DADO FOR FIXED SHELF — 7/16 — **b.** — ½ — ¼ — RABBET FOR BACK — **c.**

Router Fence Alignment

When routing a dado across a wide panel, I usually mark the location of the dado first. Then I clamp a fence parallel to the layout lines to guide the router.

The problem is trying to figure out the *exact* location of the fence. You have to measure the distance from the edge of the router base to the cutting edge of the bit, then transfer this measurement to the workpiece. Somewhere there's likely to be an error.

To be a little more accurate, I made a simple gauge. It's just a piece of scrap with a dado cut across it to align the fence

parallel to the layout lines; see Fig. 2.

To make the gauge, clamp a piece of scrap to the bench and clamp a higher fence at one end; see Fig. 1. Now mount the bit in the router and run the router base against the

high fence to rout a dado across the scrap.

To use the gauge, turn it over on the workpiece so the dado aligns with the layout lines. Then butt the fence against the end of the gauge and clamp it down; see Fig. 2. Now rout

along the edge of the fence. The dado should match the layout lines.

Since router bases can be mounted off center in relation to the bit, always keep the router facing the same direction that it was when you routed the gauge.

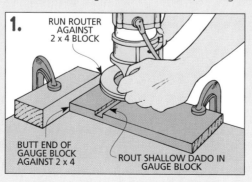

1. RUN ROUTER AGAINST 2 x 4 BLOCK — BUTT END OF GAUGE BLOCK AGAINST 2 x 4 — ROUT SHALLOW DADO IN GAUGE BLOCK

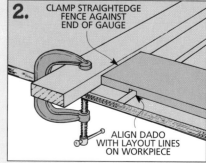

2. CLAMP STRAIGHTEDGE FENCE AGAINST END OF GAUGE — ALIGN DADO WITH LAYOUT LINES ON WORKPIECE

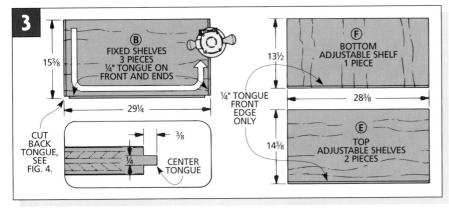

3 — FIXED SHELVES 3 PIECES ¼" TONGUE ON FRONT AND ENDS — B

15⅜

29¼

CUT BACK TONGUE, SEE FIG. 4.

⅜ / ¼ — CENTER TONGUE

¼" TONGUE FRONT EDGE ONLY

13½

28⅜

F — BOTTOM ADJUSTABLE SHELF 1 PIECE

14⅜

E — TOP ADJUSTABLE SHELVES 2 PIECES

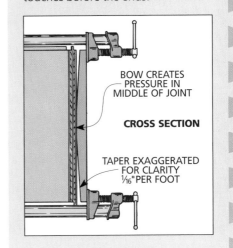

4 — PIVOT HINGE

¹¹⁄₃₂"-DIA. ¼" DEEP — BUSHING

⅞

¼

CUT BACK TONGUE ½" ON BOTH ENDS, ALL FIXED SHELVES

½

NOTE: DRILL HINGE HOLES IN BOTTOM SHELF ONLY

SHELVES

After the case sides are finished, work can begin on the shelves. There are three fixed shelves (B), two top adjustable shelves (E), and one bottom adjustable shelf (F). I started by cutting all six of these shelves to size; see Fig. 3.

TONGUES. After the shelves are cut to size, tongues are routed on the *front edges* of all the shelves for the edging strips; see Fig. 3. Next, rout tongues on both *ends* of the fixed shelves (B) only. These tongues fit into the dadoes in the case sides; see Fig. 1.

There's one more step on the tongues. The tongues on the front edge of the fixed shelves have to be trimmed back to allow space for the edging that's applied to the case sides. Trim the tongues ½" on both ends; see Fig. 4.

HOLES FOR PIVOT HINGES. Later, when the doors are hung, I used pivot hinges to mount them, refer to Fig. 4. The only problem with these hinges is that you have to drill the holes in the

bottom fixed shelf (B) before the case is assembled. If you don't drill these holes now, you can't get the drill close to the corner after assembly.

Also, these holes must be drilled in the right location for the doors to swing properly; see Fig. 4. After marking the locations as shown, drill the holes at both ends of the shelf to accept the bushings for the hinges.

ASSEMBLE THE CASE

Once the shelves were made, I began to assemble the case. I started by getting three clamps in position on the floor, spacing them so they would be in line with the dadoes; see Fig. 5. Then stand the sides on edge with the fixed shelves (B) loosely in place. (You may want to call in an assistant at this point.)

Shop Tip: To get even clamping pressure across the whole joint, I made some

tapered clamping blocks. (For more information, see the box below.) When using these blocks, I put a small piece of double-sided carpet tape on the clamp heads to hold the blocks in place.

When the clamps and tapered blocks are in place, remove one shelf and apply glue in the dado. Then clamp the shelf in place, checking for square against the sides with a framing square. Clamp the other two fixed shelves using the same procedure.

As the clamps are tightened, make sure the front shoulders of the tongues on the shelves are flush with the shoulders of the tongues on the case sides.

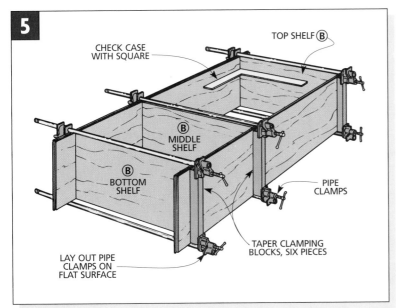

5
CHECK CASE WITH SQUARE
TOP SHELF B
MIDDLE SHELF B
BOTTOM SHELF B
PIPE CLAMPS
TAPER CLAMPING BLOCKS, SIX PIECES
LAY OUT PIPE CLAMPS ON FLAT SURFACE

Tapered Blocks

To get even pressure on the entire joint, I made tapered clamping blocks from 2x2 scrap. I used a plane (a belt sander will also work) to create a bowed shape. You don't have to work too hard — about ¹⁄₁₆" per foot is enough. It just has to bow enough so the middle touches before the ends.

BOW CREATES PRESSURE IN MIDDLE OF JOINT

CROSS SECTION

TAPER EXAGGERATED FOR CLARITY ¹⁄₁₆" PER FOOT

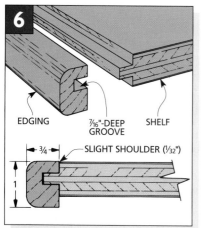

6

EDGING | 7/16"-DEEP GROOVE | SHELF

3/4 | SLIGHT SHOULDER (1/32")

1

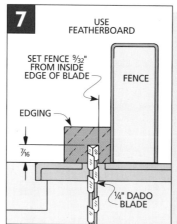

7

USE FEATHERBOARD

SET FENCE 9/32" FROM INSIDE EDGE OF BLADE

FENCE

EDGING

7/16

1/4" DADO BLADE

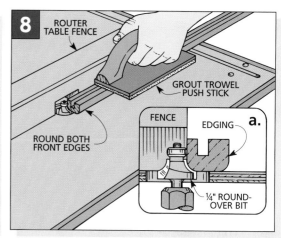

8

ROUTER TABLE FENCE

GROUT TROWEL PUSH STICK

ROUND BOTH FRONT EDGES

FENCE | EDGING | **a.**

1/4" ROUND-OVER BIT

EDGING

While the case was drying, I cut 12 edging strips: four strips for the top and bottom case edges (H), two for the front edges (I), and six for the shelves (J,K).

CUT EDGING. Start by ripping 1"-wide strips from 3/4"-thick stock. Then cut the twelve pieces to rough length.

OFF-CENTER GROOVE. Next, cut grooves in each strip to fit over the tongues on the case sides and shelves; see Fig. 6. Since the edging is 1" wide and the plywood is only 3/4" thick, the grooves are cut slightly off-center. This produces a lip on the inside of the case sides and on the bottom of the shelves.

To cut the groove, I used a dado blade on the table saw set 7/16" deep; see Fig. 7. (The groove is 1/16" deeper than the tongue to allow a glue relief.) Position the groove so the edging will stick just a hair (about 1/32") above the face of the plywood when it's glued in place; see Fig. 6. Later, you can trim this slight shoulder flush with the plywood. (I used a flush trim jig; see page 59.)

PROFILE EDGES. After the grooves are cut, round over the front edges of all the edging strips with a 1/4" roundover bit on the router table; see Fig. 8a.

Shop Note: Since these edging strips are fairly narrow, I used a grout trowel to safely rout these pieces; see Fig. 8.

CUT TO LENGTH. After making the edging strips, I cut them all to length. First cut the top and bottom strips (H) so the ends align with the shoulders of the tongues on the sides; see Fig. 9a.

Next, cut the front strips (I) that go on the front edges of the sides. Then round over the ends. Also, since the groove extends through the top end, cut a plug to fit this hole; see Fig. 9a.

Now, cut the shelf edging (J and K) to length, round over the ends, and glue it onto the shelves. Note that the lip on the top shelf faces up. The lips on the middle and bottom shelves face down.

SHELF HOLES

Once the edge strips were glued on, I drilled holes for the pin supports used to mount the top adjustable shelves (E). To position the holes, I cut a drilling template to fit between the top and middle shelves. Then I drilled 1/4" holes, spaced as shown on page 51.

After drilling the holes in the upper part of the wall unit, trim the template down to drill the holes in the lower part.

BACK, TOP, AND BASE

The basic cabinet is completed by adding the case back and the top and bottom panels.

Cut the back (D) out of 1/4" plywood so it fits snugly between the rabbets on back of the case sides, and flush with the top and bottom fixed shelves; see Fig. 10. Then screw it into the rabbets.

TOP AND BOTTOM PANELS. Next

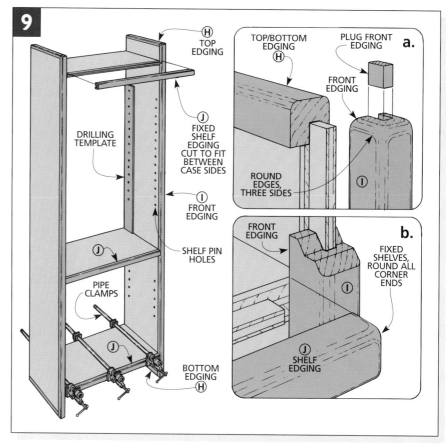

9

(H) TOP EDGING

(J) FIXED SHELF EDGING CUT TO FIT BETWEEN CASE SIDES

(I) FRONT EDGING

DRILLING TEMPLATE

SHELF PIN HOLES

(J)

(J)

PIPE CLAMPS

(J)

BOTTOM EDGING (H)

TOP/BOTTOM EDGING (H) | PLUG FRONT EDGING | **a.**

FRONT EDGING

ROUND EDGES, THREE SIDES

(I)

FRONT EDGING | **b.**

FIXED SHELVES, ROUND ALL CORNER ENDS

(I)

(J) SHELF EDGING

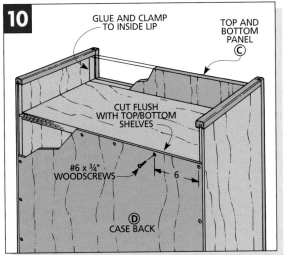

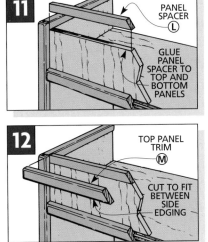

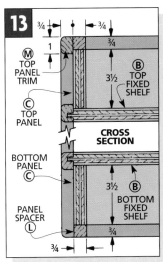

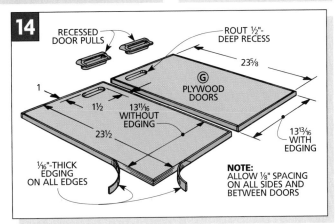

comes the top and bottom panels (C). The panels are glued to fit behind the lips of the edging strips; see Fig. 10. Note that the grain direction on these panels runs vertically.

SPACERS. To complete these panels, I added edging pieces made to look like all the other edging. To do this, first add spacers (L) to the top edge of the top panel and bottom edge of the bottom panel; see Figs. 11 and 13.

Now, on the top panel only, cut a top panel trim strip (M) 1" wide (to duplicate the look of the edging) and round over the front edges and ends with a $1/4$" roundover bit. Then glue this trim strip to the front of the spacer; see Fig. 12.

DOORS

The cabinet is complete at this point and could be used as it is. However, I added doors (G) to the bottom.

DOOR SIZES. To determine the height of the doors, measure between the *edging strips* on the two lower shelves. Then subtract $1/4$" for the $1/8$" space above and below the doors, and subtract another $1/8$" for the $1/16$"-thick edging strips that trim the doors.

To determine the width of the doors, measure between the edging strips on the case sides, subtract $3/8$" (for the $1/8$" spaces on each side of the doors and the one between the doors), and subtract $1/4$" for the edging strips. Then divide by two and cut the doors to width.

EDGING STRIPS. After cutting the doors to size, I cut $1/16$"-thick edging strips to cover all four edges of the doors. (See box below.)

After the strips are cut, glue and clamp the strips on the side edges of the doors first. Then add the strips on the top and bottom edges. Finally, trim the edges flush with the faces of the doors.

Thin Edging Strips

To safely cut thin strips I rip them off the waste side of the stock. And to cut them to a uniform thickness, I use a simple stop system. On the edge of the stop there's a "fine tuning" screw.

To use the stop, move it alongside the blade and adjust the screw until the distance between the blade and the screw equals the thickness of the strip.

Now secure the stop 3" in front of the blade.

Next, slide the work-piece against the screw. And then slide the fence against the workpiece. Lock down the fence and cut off a strip. To cut strips exactly the same width, slide the workpiece and fence against the screw again and reset the fence.

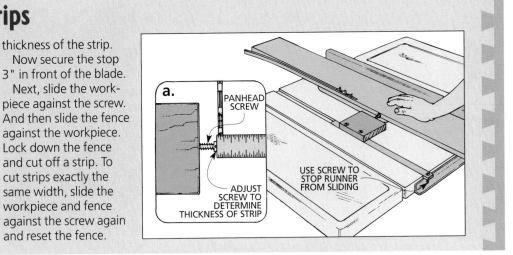

HARDWARE

The last steps are to mount the hardware on the wall unit.

PULLS. I started by cutting recesses and mounting the pulls. Since I only had two recesses to rout, I did them freehand. The pulls have a $3/32$"-wide lip around the outside — that's enough room to allow some minor variations.

I began by laying out the position of the recesses on the workpiece; refer to Fig. 14. Now, set a pull inside the lines and draw the round ends; see Fig. 15.

To rout out most of the recess, mount a straight bit and set it to depth to align with the *thickest* part of the pull; see Fig. 16. (Note: On the pulls I used, the back was sanded at an angle. So the distance from the lip to the back of the pull was inconsistent.) Now, turn on the router and plunge the bit into the center of the layout lines. Slowly clean out the waste in a clockwise direction from the center to the layout lines; see Fig. 17.

After most of the waste is cleared out with a router, switch to a chisel to clean out to the layout line; see Fig. 18. The lip is wider on the ends of the pull, so you don't have to chisel out a perfect radius.

HINGES. The doors are mounted between the two lower shelves with pivot hinges. The holes for these hinges

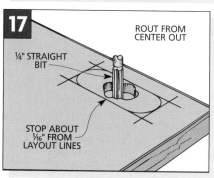

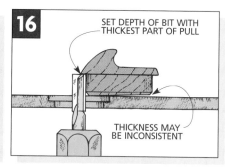

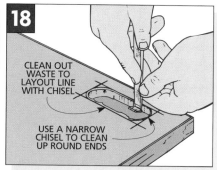

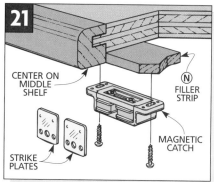

are already drilled in the bottom shelf.

As for the top holes, you need to add a filler strip (N) first; see Fig. 19. Cut this strip to fit, then drill the holes in the same position as on the bottom shelf; see Fig. 19a.

Then mount the hinges and screw them to the doors; see Fig. 20. I also mounted a magnetic catch underneath the middle fixed shelf; see Fig. 21.

LEVELERS. Although the wall unit may be perfectly level, the floor it rests on may not be — especially if there's a tack strip under the carpet near the wall. To level it, I added two adjustable levelers behind the bottom panel; see Fig. 22. The adjustment for these levelers is through a hole in the bottom shelf. Finally, there's a plug that comes with the leveler to cover this hole. ■

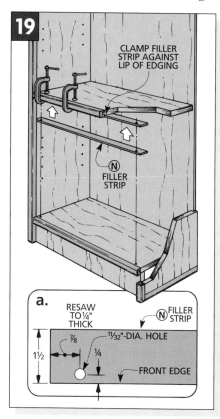

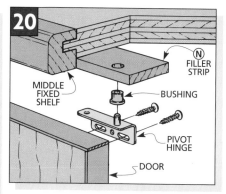

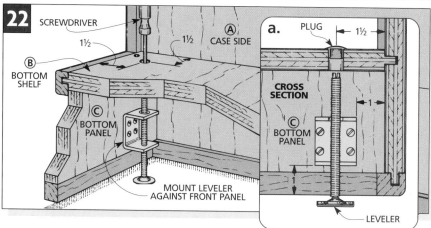

Unfortunately, the beauty of plywood is only skin deep. It's nice to work with plywood when a project calls for large pieces, but you have to cover the edges to hide the plies.

Covering the edges is usually thought of as just a cosmetic coverup. But besides hiding the ply layers, there's a good design reason for adding edging to plywood.

On many projects the plywood will look too thin if edging isn't added. For example, on the wall unit the sides are over 6 feet high, yet only 3/4" thick — a little out of proportion.

The solution is to add solid edging to the plywood. By adding a 1"-wide strip to the plywood, the piece looks thicker and more in proportion. (It also allows you to round over the edges.)

TONGUE AND GROOVE

When I want to apply solid-wood edging strips to plywood, I use a tongue and groove joint. But why not just glue the strips right on the edge? The answer has to do with alignment.

ALIGNMENT. When you start dealing with long strips, and try to get the edge of the strip aligned with the face of the plywood, it can lead to headaches. As the clamps are tightened, the edging will tend to slip on the glue.

If the edging slips down below the face of the plywood, you'll see the exposed edge. To prevent this, I align the edging just slightly (1/32") *above* the face of the plywood; see photo above.

This little lip ensures the edging strip covers the edge of the plywood completely, even if there are variations in the thickness of the plywood. Also, by creating this lip, you don't have to try to get the edging to fit exactly flush with

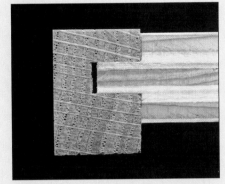

the face of the plywood. After the edging is glued on, you can come back and trim off the lip so it's perfectly flush.

Trimming off this lip is easier than it sounds. On small pieces, I use a hand plane or scraper. If I'm working with large pieces, I use a router with a flush trim bit; see page 59.

TONGUE OR GROOVE FIRST? The easiest way to align the edging to get this 1/32" lip is to use a tongue and groove joint. That is, cut a tongue on the edge of the plywood, and cut a groove down the edging strip to fit over the tongue. But which do you cut first, the tongue or the groove?

PROBLEMS. Most of the fitting problems stem from cutting the groove, because you have to be concerned about both the *width* of the groove (to fit the tongue) and the *position* of the groove (to form the lip).

So, go ahead and cut the grooves in all the edging strips first, right? Well, you could do that, but once the grooves are cut, you're committed to the position of the groove. That is, you won't know if it's in the right position to create that little lip until after the tongue is cut.

So, cut the tongues first? Well, if you cut the tongues first, and then cut the grooves later with a dado blade, you

have to make sure the tongue fits the exact width of the groove — but the groove isn't cut yet, so you can't check.

It's a problem either way. So what I do is cut both of them first. That is, I cut the actual tongue on the plywood first. But, I also set up the dado blade and cut a groove in a test piece to test the fit of the tongue.

CUTTING THE TONGUE

Although the tongue can be cut on a table saw, I think you get the best results with a router. Router bits don't usually splinter the plywood as much.

If I'm working with small pieces, I use a router table, sliding the workpiece against the fence. With large pieces I use a hand-held router. It's a whole lot easier to handle a router on a large piece of plywood than having to man-handle the sheet on a router table.

ROUT RABBETS. To make a tongue, just rout a rabbet on each face of the plywood. Since you're working from both faces with an identical setting on the router, the resulting tongue will be perfectly centered on the thickness.

ROUTER BIT. Okay, let's back up a minute. Since you're going to be routing rabbets, there are two ways to go about it: use a rabbet bit with a ball-bearing pilot or, use a straight bit with an edge guide attachment on the router.

RABBET BIT. The rabbet bit (see Fig. 1) is the quickest to set up, but may not give the best results. Often the pilot hits a little void in the core plies or runs over a little splinter on the edge. If that happens, the shoulder of the rabbet gets a little bump in it.

EDGE GUIDE. Although it takes longer to set up, I like to use an edge guide on the router; see Fig. 2.

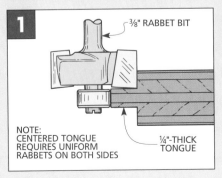

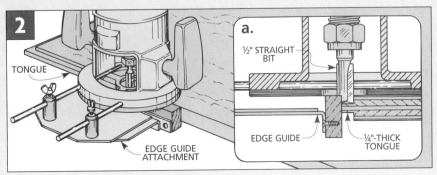

1 3/8" RABBET BIT

NOTE: CENTERED TONGUE REQUIRES UNIFORM RABBETS ON BOTH SIDES

1/4"-THICK TONGUE

2 TONGUE

EDGE GUIDE ATTACHMENT

a. 1/2" STRAIGHT BIT

EDGE GUIDE

1/4"-THICK TONGUE

When using an edge guide and a straight bit, the edge guide smoothes over any bumps or dips in the plywood edge. (For a $3/8$"-wide rabbet, I use a $1/2$" straight bit so I'm sure to clear away all the waste in one pass.)

To make the tongue on the edge of the plywood, set up the edge guide to rout a $3/8$"-wide rabbet. Then the depth has to be set. This is when you need the test piece with the groove in it.

Use a dado blade on the table saw to cut a groove in a piece of scrap. Then set the depth of cut on the router and rout rabbets on both faces of a piece of scrap plywood. (Make sure the scrap is from the same sheet as the "real" pieces.)

Gradually adjust the depth of cut, making cuts on both faces until the resulting tongue fits the groove. When the tongue fits the groove, rout rabbets on both faces of the "real" pieces.

As each tongue is completed, use the test piece to check the fit in the groove. Run the test piece down the length of the tongue to see if there's a tight area. If you hit a thick spot, rout back over that area, or clean it up with a chisel.

CUTTING THE GROOVE

After the tongue is formed on the edges of the plywood, I cut the edging strips to width and to rough length (about 2" long). Then I set up the table saw to cut the groove in the edging. There are three things to consider here.

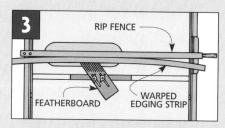

First, the width of the groove must match the thickness of the tongue you've just cut. That's taken care of with the test groove.

Second, the depth of the groove should be a little ($1/16$") deeper than the length of the tongue. This allows the shoulders to "bottom out" before the tongue hits the bottom of the groove.

Finally, the groove has to be located so the face of the edging sticks up about $1/32$" above the face of the plywood.

POSITION GROOVE. To get the groove in that position, it's basically a matter of sneaking up on the cut. To get close, measure the size of the shoulder above the tongue. Then set the fence that distance from the blade, plus $1/32$".

Now make a test cut, cutting a groove in a piece of scrap first. Then

hold the groove on the tongue on the edge of the plywood. You should be able to feel the slight lip on the top edge. Slide it along all the tongues to make sure you feel the lip everywhere. If you don't, move the fence *away* from the blade just a hair more and cut another test groove.

The idea is to feel that little $1/32$" lip. When the groove on the test piece checks out, you can work on the real edging strips.

WARPED PIECES. As you start, look for any warp in the edging strips. It makes things a little more difficult if a strip is warped, but it will still work because the tongue and groove joint will force the strip into position.

If a strip is warped, face the bowed edge toward the fence; see Fig. 3. Then use a featherboard to force the strip against the fence as the groove is cut.

TEST FIT. As each groove is cut, test its fit on the plywood edge. If it's too tight, don't change the fence until grooves are cut in all the pieces. Then move the fence away from the blade slightly and make another pass. This widens the groove, but keeps the same lip on the top edge.

After the grooves are cut, the edging strips can be glued and clamped to the edge of the plywood; see below.

How To Clamp Edging To Plywood

The problem with most pipe clamps (and bar clamps) is that they apply pressure too high up. The pressure is applied in line with the screw on the clamp head, which on most pipe clamps is centered about $5/8$" to $3/4$" above the surface of the pipe.

This can be a problem when you're gluing 1"-wide edging to $3/4$"-thick plywood, or even in the usual practice of edge-gluing $3/4$"-thick stock together.

If I'm gluing an edging strip to plywood, I lay the clamps on a flat surface and push the workpieces down against the pipes. However, as the clamps are tightened, the clamping pressure will be applied at the top edge of the edging strip; see Fig. 1. This causes the edging strip to twist so the bottom edge pulls away from the plywood.

One solution is to make a clamping board with round edges. The round edges redistribute the force of the clamp so it's centered on the thickness

of the clamping board; see Fig. 2.

To clamp edging to $3/4$" plywood, I rip a clamping board out of $3/4$"-thick stock and round over all four edges with a $3/8$" roundover bit.

THIN STRIPS. When gluing on thin strips (such as the $1/16$"-thick strips on the doors of the wall unit), I make a

slight alteration. These strips are so thin that if all the pressure is at the center, the top and bottom won't get enough pressure.

So, I make the clamping board with only one round edge which is placed against the clamp head. The flat edge goes against the thin strip; see Fig. 3.

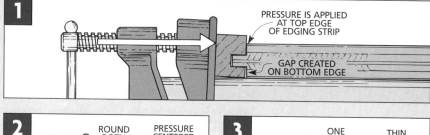

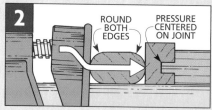

SHOP JIG .... *Flush Trim Jig*

Whenever you use wooden edging strips on plywood (or plastic laminate), you have the problem of how to trim the edging down so it's flush. Using a router with a flush trim bit is probably the easiest method. But, there can be a problem. It's difficult to balance the router on the narrow edging strip without having it tip and creating an angled cut.

To prevent this, I designed a flush trim jig. It's actually an "outrigger" that's screwed to the bottom of the router.

NEW BASE. To make the jig, begin by making a base plate (A) from $1/4$" hardboard. First, cut the base plate 7" x 7"; see Fig. 1. Then use your router's plastic base plate as a template to lay out the bit hole and the screw holes.

Now drill the holes, counterboring the screw holes to keep the screws below the surface of the plate; see Fig. 2.

SUPPORT RAILS. After making the base plate, I cut two support rails (B) to size from $3/4$" stock; see Fig. 3. Also, cut two $1/8$" kerfs $3/4$" from the end of these rails. These kerfs are used to mount the end support (C) and permit alignment of the bit.

Now, screw the support rails to the base plate; see Fig. 3. Then screw the base plate to the router using the original router screws; see Fig. 4. To keep the chips from flying in my face, I added a $1/4$" plastic chip shield; see Fig. 4.

END SUPPORT. The last piece to make is the end support (C). This controls the angle of the router bit and acts as a handle. Cut this piece to fit between the support rails; see Fig. 5. Then glue a $1\frac{1}{4}$"-wide grip on the top edge.

SET UP JIG. To set up for routing, mount a flush trim bit in the router. Then hold a square along the cutting edge of the bit and align the bottom edge of the end support; see Fig. 5. When the end support is aligned, tighten panhead screws into the kerfs.

USING THE JIG. To use the jig, adjust the bit depth so the cutting edge is only on the edging. Then place the jig on the workpiece so it rides on the bit's pilot and the end support; see Fig. 6.

Now turn on the router and pull it toward you, concentrating on keeping pressure down on the *handle*, not on the router. If the bit is cutting at an angle, raise or lower the support; see Fig. 6.

1

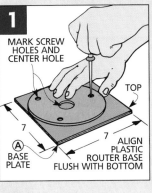

MARK SCREW HOLES AND CENTER HOLE

TOP

7

7 ALIGN PLASTIC ROUTER BASE FLUSH WITH BOTTOM

Ⓐ BASE PLATE

2

COUNTERBORE SCREWHEADS BELOW SURFACE

BIT HOLE

TOP

BOTTOM

3

Ⓑ SUPPORT RAIL

$1/8$" KERF

Ⓑ SUPPORT RAIL

$2\frac{1}{2}$

10

$3/4$

$3/4$

SCREW SUPPORT RAILS FLUSH WITH TOP CORNERS OF BASE PLATE

#8 x $3/4$" Fh WOODSCREWS

Ⓑ

4

SCREW BASE PLATE TO ROUTER WITH ORIGINAL SCREWS

#6 x $3/4$" SCREWS

SCREW DOWN PLEXIGLAS CHIP SHIELD FLUSH WITH SUPPORT RAILS

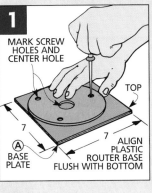

5

END SUPPORT Ⓒ

SQUARE END SUPPORT WITH CUTTING EDGE OF BIT

$1\frac{1}{4}$"-WIDE GRIP

#8 x $1\frac{1}{4}$" PANHEAD SCREWS

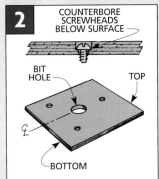
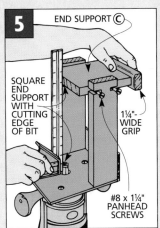

6

CHIP SHIELD

Ⓐ

Ⓒ

Ⓑ

ADJUST SUPPORT RAILS UNTIL BIT ALIGNS WITH WORK SURFACE

END OF JIG TOO HIGH

END OF JIG TOO LOW

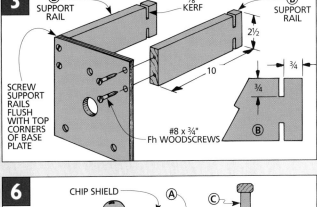
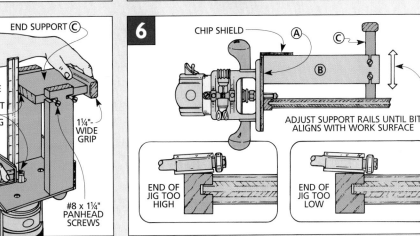

OAK BOOKCASE

Assembled with frames and panels, this bookcase is a strong and beautiful place to hold a growing home library.

Although a bookcase doesn't have to be fancy to do its job, it ought to get more respect than the old "boards and bricks" approach. This bookcase not only looks great, but it's strong as well.

One reason that it's so strong is that I built it from red oak. But there's another reason that you can't see right away — the joinery.

JOINERY. I used a variety of joints, each one designed to add strength to a different part of the project.

First, the sides and back are frames and panels assembled with stub tenons

and grooves. Then the three frame units are joined together with rabbets and grooves.

Next, stopped sliding dovetail joints hold the apron that spans between the side frames.

The top and bottom are made from ¾" oak plywood held within a mitered frame. And the base pieces are connected with yet another strong joint — a splined miter.

Finally, there's a bullnose edging strip added to the front of the ¾" plywood shelf with a classic tongue and groove joint.

SHELF REINFORCEMENT. There's one other thing that I did to add strength to this bookcase.

Over time, shelves filled with books can start to droop like a swaybacked horse. I don't think the shelf in this bookcase ever will. That's because it's reinforced with oak strips that run *under* the length of the shelf. (For more on reinforcing shelves, see page 94.)

FINISH. Once all of the joints were cut and the project assembled, I finished it with two coats of Minwax Early American stain and then applied two coats of tung oil for protection.

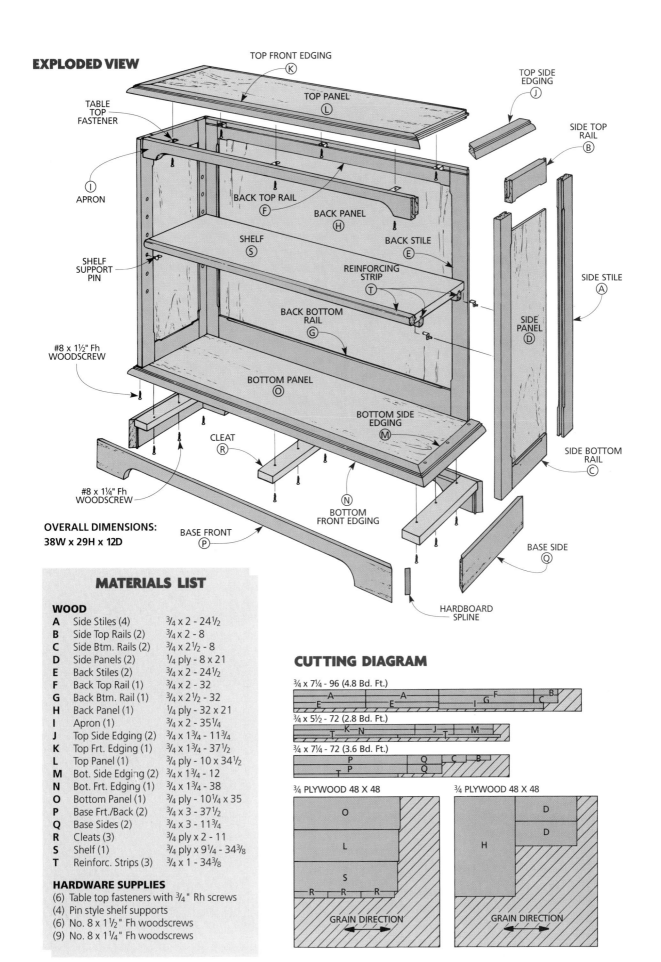

EXPLODED VIEW

TOP FRONT EDGING
(K)

TOP PANEL
(L)

TOP SIDE EDGING
(J)

TABLE TOP FASTENER

SIDE TOP RAIL
(B)

(I)

APRON

BACK TOP RAIL
(F)

BACK PANEL
(H)

SIDE STILE
(A)

SHELF
(S)

BACK STILE
(E)

SHELF SUPPORT PIN

REINFORCING STRIP
(T)

SIDE PANEL
(D)

BACK BOTTOM RAIL
(G)

#8 x 1½" Fh WOODSCREW

BOTTOM PANEL
(O)

BOTTOM SIDE EDGING
(M)

CLEAT
(R)

SIDE BOTTOM RAIL
(C)

#8 x 1¼" Fh WOODSCREW

BOTTOM FRONT EDGING
(N)

OVERALL DIMENSIONS:
38W x 29H x 12D

BASE FRONT
(P)

BASE SIDE
(Q)

HARDBOARD SPLINE

MATERIALS LIST

WOOD

A	Side Stiles (4)	¾ x 2 - 24½
B	Side Top Rails (2)	¾ x 2 - 8
C	Side Btm. Rails (2)	¾ x 2½ - 8
D	Side Panels (2)	¼ ply - 8 x 21
E	Back Stiles (2)	¾ x 2 - 24½
F	Back Top Rail (1)	¾ x 2 - 32
G	Back Btm. Rail (1)	¾ x 2½ - 32
H	Back Panel (1)	¼ ply - 32 x 21
I	Apron (1)	¾ x 2 - 35¼
J	Top Side Edging (2)	¾ x 1¾ - 11¾
K	Top Frt. Edging (1)	¾ x 1¾ - 37½
L	Top Panel (1)	¾ ply - 10 x 34½
M	Bot. Side Edging (2)	¾ x 1¾ - 12
N	Bot. Frt. Edging (1)	¾ x 1¾ - 38
O	Bottom Panel (1)	¾ ply - 10¼ x 35
P	Base Frt./Back (2)	¾ x 3 - 37½
Q	Base Sides (2)	¾ x 3 - 11¾
R	Cleats (3)	¾ ply x 2 - 11
S	Shelf (1)	¾ ply x 9¼ - 34⅜
T	Reinforc. Strips (3)	¾ x 1 - 34⅜

HARDWARE SUPPLIES

(6) Table top fasteners with ¾" Rh screws
(4) Pin style shelf supports
(6) No. 8 x 1½" Fh woodscrews
(9) No. 8 x 1¼" Fh woodscrews

CUTTING DIAGRAM

¾ x 7¼ - 96 (4.8 Bd. Ft.)

A A F B
E E I G C

¾ x 5½ - 72 (2.8 Bd. Ft.)

T K N J T M

¾ x 7¼ - 72 (3.6 Bd. Ft.)

P Q C B
T P Q

¾ PLYWOOD 48 X 48

O
L
S
R R R

GRAIN DIRECTION

¾ PLYWOOD 48 X 48

D
D
H

GRAIN DIRECTION

FRAMES

I started construction by making the two side frames and the back frame.

Begin by ripping all the bottom rails (C and G) $2\frac{1}{2}$" wide; see Fig. 1. Then adjust the fence to rip the top rails (B and F) and stiles (A and E) 2" wide. Now cut the pieces to final length.

EDGE GROOVES. After all the pieces are cut to size, they're ready for the tongue and groove joints that hold them together. The grooves are centered on the inside edge of all the frame pieces. (These grooves accept $\frac{1}{4}$" *hardwood* plywood which is usually thinner than $\frac{1}{4}$." So cut the grooves to fit the actual thickness of the plywood.)

To cut the centered grooves, position the fence so the blade is slightly off center; see Fig. 2. Then cut a $\frac{1}{2}$"-deep kerf the length of the workpiece. Now flip it end-for-end and make a second pass. This produces a centered groove.

SIDE GROOVES. After cutting the grooves on the inside edges, another set of grooves is cut to join the back frame to the side frames. These grooves are cut on the inside face of the side frame's rear stiles (A); see Fig. 4.

It's important that these grooves be positioned so the distance from the back edge of the stile to the far side of the groove is equal to the thickness of the back frame's stile; see Fig. 4a.

STUB TENON. The tongues that connect the ends of the rails to the stiles are actually stub tenons that fit into the panel grooves; see Fig. 3.

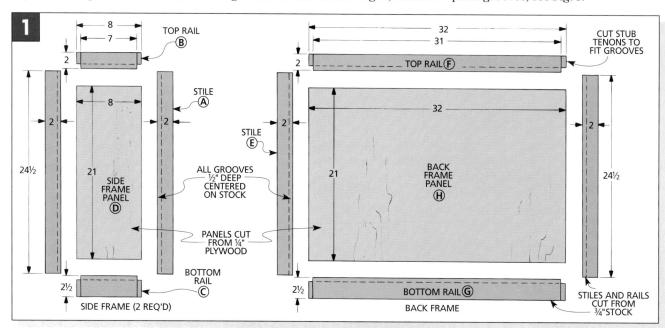

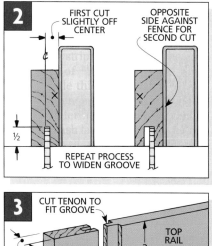

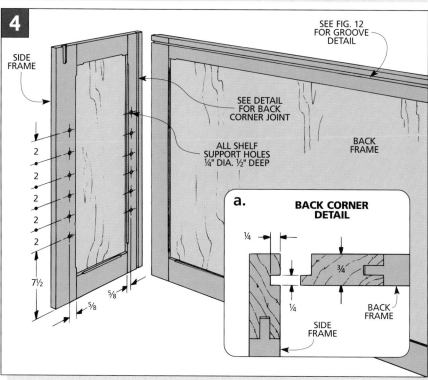

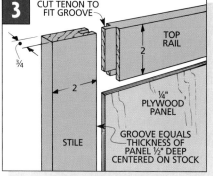

These stub tenons are cut by making multiple passes over the saw blade to leave a tongue that fits the groove.

PLYWOOD PANELS. After the stub tenons are cut, dry-assemble the frames and take measurements for the plywood panels. Then cut the panels to size making sure the grain runs the height of the case; see Fig. 1.

BACK FRAME TONGUES. Before gluing up the frames, I also cut the tongues on the back frame stiles that join the side frames; see Fig. 4a.

ASSEMBLE PANELS. Now each of the three frame and panel assemblies can be glued up. As I was gluing up the frames, I glued the panels into the frame grooves for maximum stability.

CHAMFERS. After the assemblies dried, there are a few more steps to complete the three units. First, I routed 1/8"-wide decorative chamfers around the *inside* edges of the stiles and rails; see the tip box below.

SHELF HOLES. Next, drill holes for the shelf pins that support the center shelf; see Figs. 4 and 5.

DOVETAIL GROOVES. The last step is to rout stopped dovetail grooves in the side frames to accept a top apron (I). (This apron spans the front of the case; refer to Fig. 13 on page 64.) The grooves are located on the inside face of each front stile; see Fig. 6.

To rout the groove in the left frame,

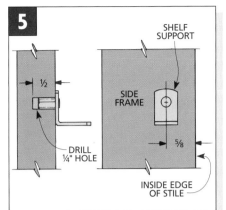

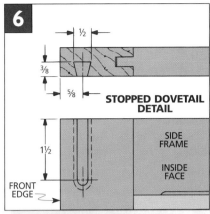

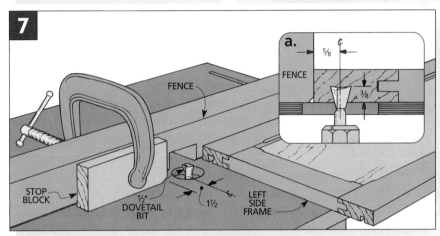

clamp a stop block to the left of the bit on the router table; see Fig. 7. For the right frame, move the stop block to the right of the bit and repeat the cut from the opposite direction.

Shop Note: After making these cuts, don't change the setting on the bit. You need it to cut the dovetail tongues later.

Inside Chamfers

If a frame and panel are already assembled it's difficult to rout a chamfer on the frame because the panel gets in the way of the pilot on the chamfering bit.

To deal with this problem, I used a "V-groove" bit instead. And to guide the bit, I made an auxiliary base and special 1 1/2"-wide guide from 1/4" hardboard; see Fig. 1.

The primary function of this guide is the same as that of the pilot on a chamfering bit. It keeps the bit a uniform distance from the edge being chamfered. But the guide also stops

the chamfer a uniform distance (3/4" in this case) from the corners.

To make the chamfer, just adjust the depth of cut. The guide will maintain a uniform chamfer and stop the cut exactly 3/4" from the corners; see Fig. 2.

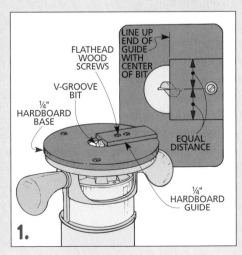

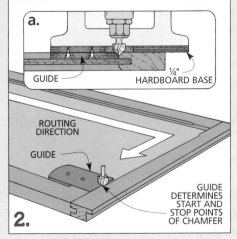

FRONT APRON

After the frames and panels were complete, I started work on the front apron; refer to Fig. 13.

CUT TO SIZE. Begin by cutting the apron (I) 2"-wide; see Fig. 8. The length of the apron equals the shoulder-to-shoulder length of the back frame (*without* the tongues), plus ³⁄₄" (for the two ³⁄₈" dovetail tongues.

DOVETAIL TENONS. To hold the apron securely while forming the dovetail tenons, I clamped it in a hand screw clamp; see Fig. 9. Then I adjusted the fence to take just a little off each face to form the tenon. Now creep up on the final thickness by moving the fence and repeat the process until the tenons fit the dovetail grooves.

Next, trim about ¹⁄₂" off the bottom of each tenon so when it slides into the groove, the top of the apron is flush with the top of the frame; see Fig. 10.

CUT PROFILE. Now the curved profile can be cut. To do this, draw a 1"-radius curve near each end; see Fig. 8. Then cut out the shape staying about ¹⁄₈" outside the pencil line.

To finish up to the line, I used the router table with a long fence and a straight bit; see Fig. 11. Make a series of light passes until the edge is straight

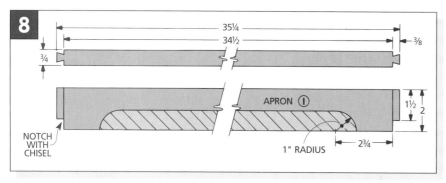

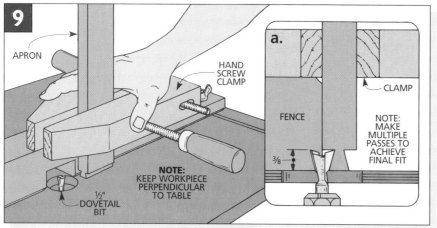

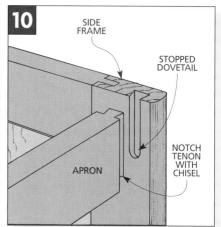

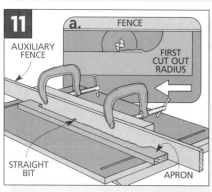

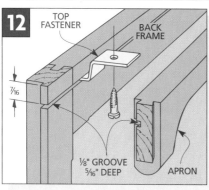

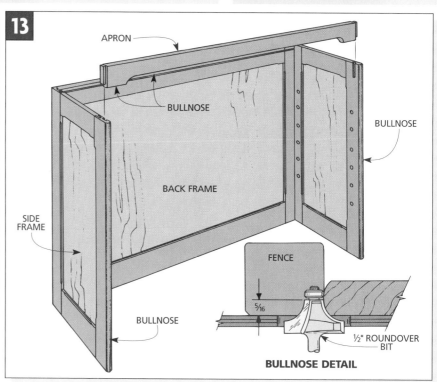

and smooth, and lines up with the radiused corners.

FASTENER GROOVES. Next it's time to plan ahead for fastening the top. I used stamped metal fasteners that fit into grooves. Cut the grooves along the inside edges of the apron and top rail of the back frame; see Fig. 12.

SOFTEN EDGES. The last step before assembling the case is softening the edges with a bullnose profile; see Detail in Fig. 13. Rout the front of the side frames and the bottom of the apron.

ASSEMBLE. Finally, the case can be assembled; see Fig. 13. First glue the side frames to the back frame. Then add the front apron.

TOP AND BOTTOM

Once the case is assembled, the top and bottom can be made. I started by cutting the two plywood panels (L and O) to size; see Fig. 14.

Shop Note: The top frame hangs over the case $3/4''$ on the sides and front, so it should be built $3/4''$ deeper and $1 1/2''$ wider than the outside dimensions of the assembled case. The bottom frame hangs over 1", so it should be 1" deeper and 2" wider than the case.

EDGING STRIP. The back edge of the plywood is covered with a $1/4''$-thick trim strip. Rip this strip from $3/4''$ stock and glue it to the plywood.

MITERED FRAMES. Next, the mitered frames can be made. Begin by ripping the pieces $1 3/4''$ wide, see Fig. 14. These pieces are joined to the plywood with tongue and groove joints. So, cut a $1/4''$ x $1/4''$ groove centered on the inside edge of all the pieces. Then form a matching tongue on the front and sides of the plywood panels by cutting rabbets on the top and bottom faces; see Fig. 15 and the box at right.

When cutting the mitered corners, I concentrated on shaving the ends of the frame's front pieces (K and N) until the inside corners fit the inside corners of the panel; see Fig. 16. Then I mitered the ends of the frame sides (J and M), leaving the back end a little long.

RABBET. There's one more small step. Cut a tiny rabbet on the inside of the top frame pieces; see Fig. 15a. (This adds an accent line and makes the joint more forgiving than a butt joint.)

ASSEMBLY. Now glue up the frames and panels and trim the back ends of the frame pieces flush with the panel.

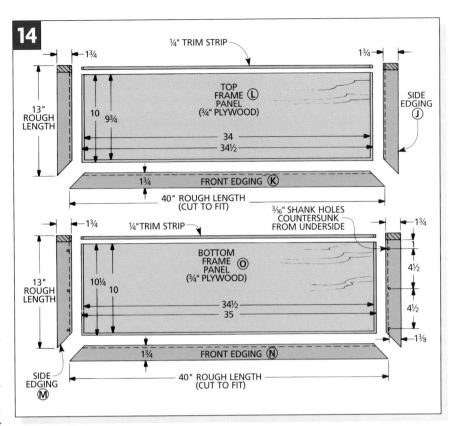

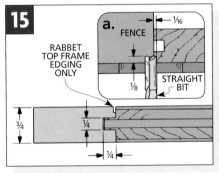

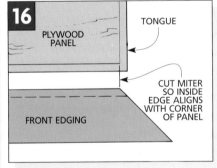

Scoring For A Smooth Rabbet

Cutting a rabbet *across* the grain on plywood almost always results in tearout along the shoulder line. The way to eliminate this is to score the edge before routing.

The problem with scoring is locating the score line *exactly* where the edge of the rabbet will be. I solved this problem by routing an identical rabbet in a strip of scrap on the router table. The strip was then used as a guide to score the plywood.

After the rabbet is routed in the strip, just fit the strip over the end of the plywood to guide an X-Acto knife while scoring. Then, flip the plywood over and rout a clean rabbet.

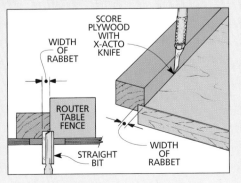

EDGE PROFILE

To dress up the edges of these frames, I wanted to make a fancy profile with a roundover bit and a core box bit. However, I ran into problems on the router table because the shank of the bit had to be pulled too far out of the collet.

A safer alternative is to work with a hand-held router so the collet can get a full grip on the bit. The problem is that when the bit projects full depth, there isn't anything for the pilot to ride on.

To solve this problem, I cut some 1/4" hardboard and fastened it with carpet tape to the underside of the frame flush with the edges; see Fig. 17. When the bit reaches full depth, the pilot rides along the hardboard; see Fig. 17a.

ROUT COVE. To complete the profile, I routed a small cove on the shoulder of the roundover; see Fig. 18.

BASE

With the basic cabinet complete, I was ready to make the base. The base is a frame joined with splined miter joints.

CUT TO SIZE. To begin, rip the sides (Q) and front and back pieces (P) to a finished width of 3" and rough length; see Fig. 19.

RABBETS. The base is attached to the case by three plywood cleats. I found the easiest way to mount these cleats was to cut a rabbet on the inside top edge of all the base pieces; see Fig. 19a.

MITER ENDS. After the rabbets are complete, cut the pieces to final length with a 45° miter on each end. Note: The length of the pieces is determined by the size of the bottom frame. The base should set back 1/4" on the front and sides and be flush on the back; refer to Figs. 23 and 27.

SPLINES. To strengthen the corners and help keep them aligned while gluing, the mitered joints are splined with strips of 1/8" hardboard. I cut the kerfs on the table saw; see Fig. 20.

BOTTOM PROFILE. Next, a curved profile can be made on the front and back pieces; see Fig. 21. I did this the same way as I did the apron (I).

CLEATS. Now dry-clamp the base and measure between the rabbets for the cleats (R); see Fig. 19.

ASSEMBLY. The base frame is assembled by gluing the corners together with the splines in place. While the glue is wet, glue the cleats in place.

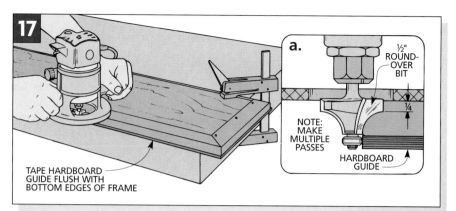

17

TAPE HARDBOARD GUIDE FLUSH WITH BOTTOM EDGES OF FRAME

a. 1/2" ROUND-OVER BIT
1/4"
NOTE: MAKE MULTIPLE PASSES
HARDBOARD GUIDE

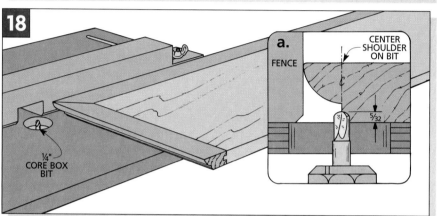

18

1/4" CORE BOX BIT

a. FENCE
CENTER SHOULDER ON BIT
5/32

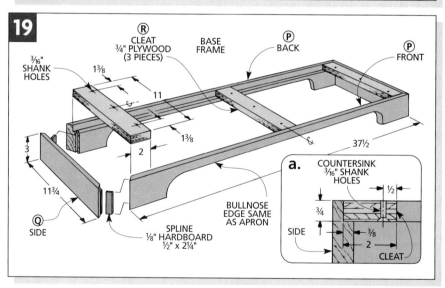

19

®CLEAT 3/4" PLYWOOD (3 PIECES)
BASE FRAME
℗ BACK
℗ FRONT
3/16" SHANK HOLES
1 3/8
11
1 3/8
37 1/2
3
2
11 3/4
Ⓠ SIDE
SPLINE 1/8" HARDBOARD 1/2" x 2 1/4"
BULLNOSE EDGE SAME AS APRON

a. COUNTERSINK 3/16" SHANK HOLES
1/2
3/4
SIDE
3/8
2
CLEAT

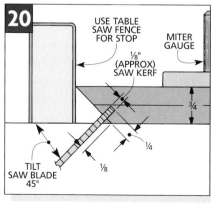

20

USE TABLE SAW FENCE FOR STOP
MITER GAUGE
1/8" (APPROX) SAW KERF
3/4
TILT SAW BLADE 45°
1/8
1/4

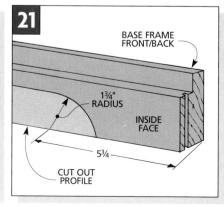

21

BASE FRAME FRONT/BACK
1 3/4" RADIUS
INSIDE FACE
CUT OUT PROFILE
5 3/4

MOUNT BOTTOM FRAME. While the base is drying, the bottom plywood frame can be fastened to the case. To do this, turn the case upside down and align the bottom frame on it; see Fig. 22.

Now glue and screw the bottom frame and case together.

MOUNT BASE FRAME. To mount the base frame, drill pilot holes and drive screws through the cleats into the plywood bottom; see Fig. 23.

MOUNT TOP. Next, the top frame can be attached with fasteners; see Fig. 24. Turn over the top frame and center the case on it. Then slip the fasteners into the grooves and screw them down.

SHELF

The shelf starts as a piece of plywood 10" wide and ⅛" less in length than the inside of the bookcase; see Fig. 26.

BULLNOSE PIECES. To keep the shelf from sagging, I added reinforcing strips (T) into ¼" grooves on the front edge and bottom face; see Fig. 26.

After cutting the grooves, rip 1"-wide strips and cut rabbets to produce a tongue that matches the grooves; see Step 1 in Fig. 25.

To complete the strips, rout a bull-nose profile on the other edges; see Step 2. Finally, glue the strips in place. ■

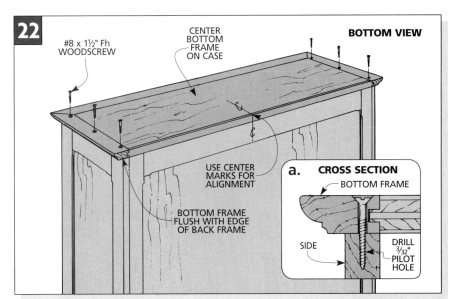

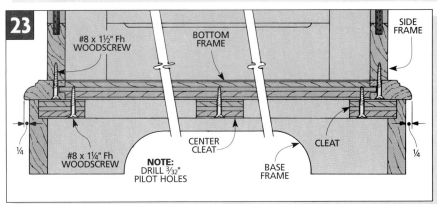

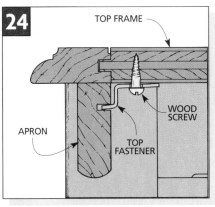

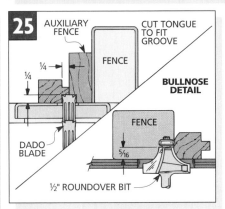

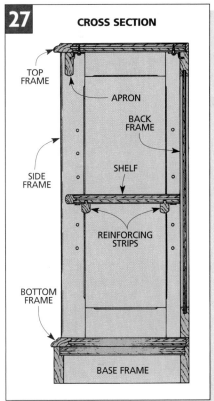

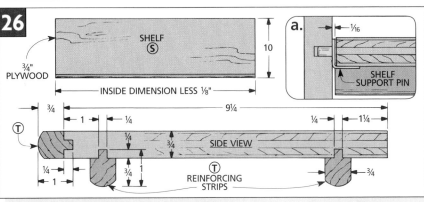

CLASSIC BOOKCASE

It's what you don't see that makes this project unique. Knock-down hardware makes it easy to assemble and convenient to move.

I've always wanted to build a large, formal-looking bookcase. But I had visions of wrestling it around my shop when the time came to assemble and finish it.

The design of this bookcase changed all that. A simple, straightforward system breaks the project down into manageable sized pieces that are easy to handle.

To see what's special about the design, you need to look inside. Here you'll find a "knock-down" system using bolts and nuts to hold things together. Not something you'd expect on a classic piece of furniture.

What makes this system work are the individual components used to build the bookcase. The base, sides, and top are all built as separate units. Once completed you just bolt them together.

And it's just as easy to take it apart. You won't need to hire a moving crew if you get tired of it in the living room.

Another benefit to using components is being able to change the overall appearance. By building a different top assembly, the project takes on a completely new look. For example, the classic top with the oval can be replaced with a straight one; see page 74.

WOOD. A classic project requires a classic wood. And tight-grained cherry and cherry plywood with its subtle grain pattern is perfect. For the back panel I used $1/4$" cherry plywood.

FINISH. When it came time to apply a finish I decided to use a cherry stain. I wanted the rich reddish-brown color without waiting for the aging process. And using stain would even out the color differences between the lighter sapwood and darker hardwood.

I stained with Bartley's Pennsylvania Cherry Gel Finish. A gel finish doesn't penetrate as deep as other stains so it isn't as likely to leave dark blotches.

After the stain dried, I wiped on three coats of Bartley's Clear Varnish.

EXPLODED VIEW

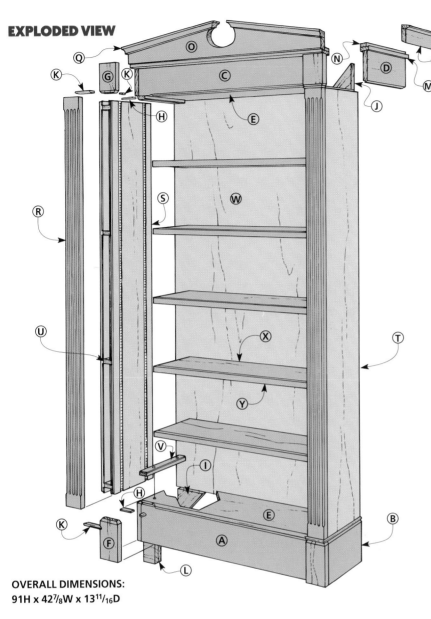

OVERALL DIMENSIONS:
91H x 42⁷/₈W x 13¹¹/₁₆D

MATERIALS LIST

WOOD

A	Lwr. Case Frt. (1)	$3/4 \times 6^5/8 - 39^5/8$
B	Lwr. Case Sides (2)	$3/4 \times 6^5/8 - 11^{13}/16$
C	Upr. Case Frt. (1)	$3/4 \times 4^5/8 - 39^5/8$
D	Upr. Case Sides (2)	$3/4 \times 4^5/8 - 11^{13}/16$
E	Top/Btm. Panls. (2)	$3/4$ ply - $11^3/16 \times 39^7/8$
F	Lwr. Case Blks. (2)	$3/4 \times 3^5/8 - 6^5/8$
G	Upr. Case Blks.(2)	$3/4 \times 3^5/8 - 4^5/8$
H	Filler Pieces (4)	$3/8 \times 3/4 - 2^1/8$
I	Lwr. Crnr. Blks. (2)	$3/4 \times 5 - 9$ rough
J	Upr. Crnr. Blks. (2)	$3/4 \times 4 - 6$ rough
K	Bead Molding (1)	$3/8 \times 5/8 - 14$ feet
L	Leveler Blocks (4)	$3/4 \times 5^3/4 - 2^1/8$
M	Top Molding (1)	$3/4 \times 1^3/4 - 78$
N	Cleat (1)	$3/4 \times 1^1/4 - 78$
O	Top Front (1)	$3/4 \times 6 - 44$ rough
P	Top Sides (2)	$3/4 \times 3 - 14$ rough
Q	Cove Molding (1)	$3/4 \times 1^3/8 - 78$
R	Fluted Caps (2)	$3/4 \times 3^3/4 - 84$ rough
S	Interior Panels (2)	$3/4$ ply - $11^1/2 \times 72$
T	Exterior Panels (2)	$3/4$ ply - $11^3/4 \times 72$
U	Ribs (8)	$3/4 \times 2 - 11^1/4$
V	Align. Blocks (4)	$3/4 \times 1^1/2 \times 11^1/4$
W	Back (1)	$1/4$ ply - $38^1/2 \times 73^1/2$
X	Shelves (5)	$3/4$ ply - $10^1/2 \times 33^{15}/16$
Y	Trim Pieces (5)	$3/4 \times 1^1/4 - 33^{15}/16$

HARDWARE SUPPLIES

(68) No. 8 x 1¼" Fh woodscrews
(8) ¼-20 x 3" Hex head bolts
(8) ¼" Flat washers
(8) ¼-20 T-nuts
(2) 1⅛"-dia. Levelers with T-nuts
(4) 72" Shelf standard brackets (brown)
(52) Bracket nails (brown)
(20) Shelf supports (brown)

CUTTING DIAGRAM

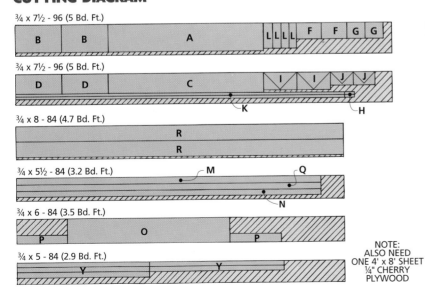

¾ x 7½ - 96 (5 Bd. Ft.)

¾ x 7½ - 96 (5 Bd. Ft.)

¾ x 8 - 84 (4.7 Bd. Ft.)

¾ x 5½ - 84 (3.2 Bd. Ft.)

¾ x 6 - 84 (3.5 Bd. Ft.)

¾ x 5 - 84 (2.9 Bd. Ft.)

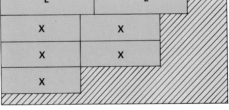

¾" CHERRY PLYWOOD 48 x 96

¾" CHERRY PLYWOOD 48 x 96

NOTE:
ALSO NEED
ONE 4' x 8' SHEET
¼" CHERRY
PLYWOOD

UPPER & LOWER CASE

This bookcase is built in separate assemblies. Normally, I'd build them one at a time. But here, the upper and lower case assemblies are almost identical. (The upper case is 2" shorter.) Building them at the same time reduced the number of setups.

FRONT & SIDES. Both the upper and lower case assemblies start with a front and two side pieces. I began by cutting the lower case front (A) and sides (B) to finished size; see Fig. 1. And then repeated the same steps to make the upper case front (C) and sides (D).

Next, I used a locking rabbet joint to hold the front and side pieces together; see Fig. 2. A tongue cut on the front pieces fits in a 1/4"-deep dado cut on the side pieces. The important thing here is to make the tongue fit snug in the dado.

After cutting the tongue, I rabbeted the top edge of the lower case assembly and the bottom edge of the upper case assembly; see Fig. 3. These rabbets will hold a top and bottom panel which are made next.

TOP/BOTTOM PANELS. To determine the length of the top/bottom panels (E), dry assemble the fronts and sides and measure the distance between the rabbets on the sides; see Fig. 4.

Then to determine the width, measure from the rabbet on both front pieces to the back edges of the sides. But you need to leave room for the plywood back (added later). So the width of each panel is cut so it's 1/4" short of the back edge; see Fig. 4a. In my case, the finished size of both top/bottom panels (E) was 11 3/16" x 39 7/8".

After the panels are cut to size, the next step is to rabbet three edges of each panel (front and side edges); see Figs. 4 and 4a. This rabbet creates a "shelf" for molding that's added later; refer to Fig. 10 on page 72.

Once both panels have been rabbeted, glue the upper/lower case sides, fronts, and panels together. Clamp the pieces and check that everything remains square.

LEVELER BLOCKS. Because the bookcase stands so tall, levelers are added to the lower case assembly to keep the back tight against the wall. To hold these levelers, I added blocks (L) at both front corners; see Fig. 5. The leveler blocks also act as glue blocks and help strengthen the corners.

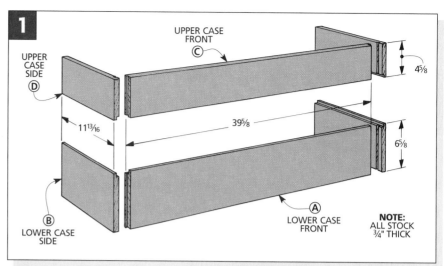

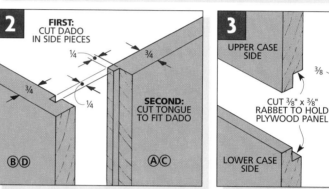

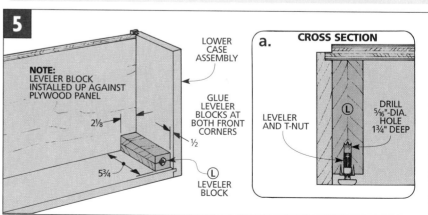

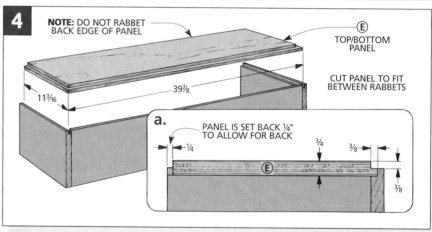

Each leveler block is glued up from two pieces of ¾"-thick stock. A T-nut is installed in one end and the levelers screw into the nut; see Fig. 5a.

When installing the blocks, position them tight against the plywood panel. Then glue and clamp them in place.

CASE BLOCKS. The next step is to add lower case blocks (F) and upper case blocks (G). The blocks cover up the end grain on the side pieces and give the bookcase a distinctive look.

Both sets of blocks are cut to the same width (3⅝"). But the height of each set is determined by the height of the upper and lower assemblies; see Fig. 6. (Note: For tight-fitting case blocks I made relief cuts on the back faces; see the tip box below.)

You might be tempted to glue the blocks directly to the front pieces. But the wood grain on the blocks runs in a different direction than the front pieces. So there's a good chance the blocks would "pop-off" if the wood moved from changes in humidity.

Instead, I drilled two shank holes through the case fronts and screwed the blocks in place; see Fig. 6a.

FILLER PIECES. Next I added filler pieces. These act as backing for bead molding that will be glued to the top of the case blocks later. I cut the hardwood filler pieces (H) ⅜"-thick and glued them in place; see Fig. 7.

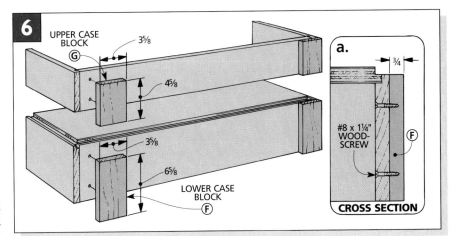

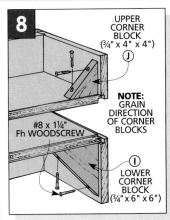

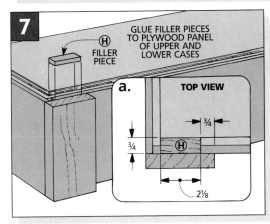

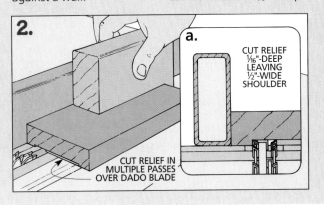

CORNER BLOCKS. Then I turned the assemblies around so I could glue and screw on lower (I) and upper (J) corner blocks at the back corners; see Fig. 8.

These triangular-shaped blocks add support to each assembly. Note: The blocks are installed flush with the back edge of the plywood.

Relief Cuts

The success of a project depends on the fit of the parts. This is especially true for a piece of trim that's applied to the face of a project such as the case blocks on this bookcase.

The blocks should fit tight to the case along their edges. But if the blocks are cupped even slightly the edges *won't* fit tight; see Fig. 1.

This is the same problem faced by carpenters who install trim molding in houses. Their solution is to use molding that's milled with a shallow "relief" on the back side to fit up tight against a wall.

So I cut a shallow channel across the back side to create relief behind the block; see Fig. 2. Note: In order to avoid weakening the block, only cut the channel 1/16" deep.

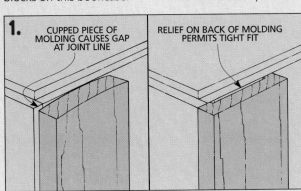

CHAMFER EDGES. After installing the corner blocks, I turned the upper and lower assemblies over and routed a chamfer around three edges; see Figs. 9 and 9a. (See the box below for tips on preventing chipout when routing.)

One problem here is that the chamfer bit won't cut a square inside corner. So to clean up the inside corners right up next to the case blocks, I used a sharp chisel and followed the profile of the bevel; see Fig. 9b.

BEAD MOLDING. The next step is to make the bead molding (K). The molding fits on the rabbeted edge on both the upper and lower cases and wraps around the filler piece; see Fig. 10.

First I cut the molding to size; see Fig. 9a. Then I used a $3/16$" roundover bit in the router table to rout a bullnose profile on the front edge of each piece. Note: I made extra molding in case I cut a piece or two that didn't quite fit.

When installing the molding, cut the long pieces first (the ones that cover the lower and upper case fronts). That way if you cut one a little short, it still can be used for the side pieces. Then work your way around to the sides, cutting and fitting the pieces as you go. Finally, glue all the pieces in place.

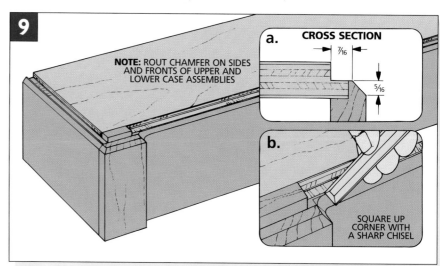

9

NOTE: ROUT CHAMFER ON SIDES AND FRONTS OF UPPER AND LOWER CASE ASSEMBLIES

a. CROSS SECTION

7/16

5/16

b. SQUARE UP CORNER WITH A SHARP CHISEL

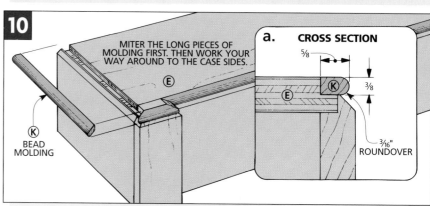

10

MITER THE LONG PIECES OF MOLDING FIRST. THEN WORK YOUR WAY AROUND TO THE CASE SIDES.

E

K
BEAD MOLDING

a. CROSS SECTION

5/8

3/8

K

E

3/16"
ROUNDOVER

Backrouting

You can run into a problem when freehand routing around a corner.

That's the situation I faced while building the bookcase. Both the upper and lower assemblies call for chamfers around the sides and front.

If you try to rout these chamfers in the normal way (feeding the router from left to right), you will be approaching the corner of the front trim piece from *behind*; see Fig. 1.

As the router bit exits the corner, it will take a chunk of wood with it; see Fig. 1a. But chipout like this can be avoided by approaching the corner from the front; see Fig. 2.

Freehand routing from right to left is called "backrouting." There are a couple things to keep in mind when backrouting.

First, keep a firm grip on the router. In the normal

feed direction, the router bit pulls itself smoothly along the workpiece.

But it's different when backrouting. Now the bit tends to "hop" taking little nibbles out of the wood.

The second tip for backrouting is to take light (shallow) passes. Again, the reason for this is control. By taking smaller nibbles, the router bit will do less hopping.

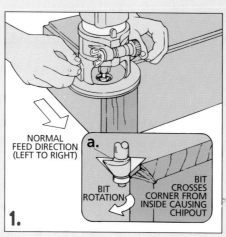

1. NORMAL FEED DIRECTION (LEFT TO RIGHT)

a. BIT ROTATION
BIT CROSSES CORNER FROM INSIDE CAUSING CHIPOUT

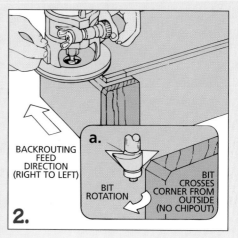

2. BACKROUTING FEED DIRECTION (RIGHT TO LEFT)

a. BIT ROTATION
BIT CROSSES CORNER FROM OUTSIDE (NO CHIPOUT)

UPPER CASE MOLDING

At this point, the lower case assembly is done, so you can set it aside for now and start work on the upper case. It's built with several layers of molding.

TOP MOLDING. The first piece is the top molding (M); see Fig. 11. The molding starts out as a single workpiece cut into three pieces. It's the base for the rest of the molding.

Installing the molding is pretty straightforward. Simply miter the pieces so the molding overhangs the sides and the case blocks on the front by $1/4$"; see Figs. 11a and 11b. Then glue and screw them in place.

CLEAT. The next "layer" added to the top assembly is the cleat (N); see Fig. 12. The $1^1/4$"-wide cleat is installed so its back edge is flush with the back edge of the top molding; see Fig. 12a. This creates a $1/2$" wide "shelf" for the next layer of molding to rest on.

TOP FRONT. Now the top front (O) can be added; see Fig. 13. (Note: For an alternate design, see page 74.)

The top front is a beveled piece of molding with two tapered sides and an oval cut out of the middle. I cut the beveled ends first; see Fig. 13a. And then marked the centerline on the length of the board.

From the center of the top front I drew an oval. (For more on drawing ovals, see the box below.) Then I marked the tapered cuts on each side of the oval.

I cut out the oval with a sabre saw close to the line and cleaned up to the line with a drum sander. Then cut the tapers and glue and clamp the top front to the cleat; see Fig. 13b.

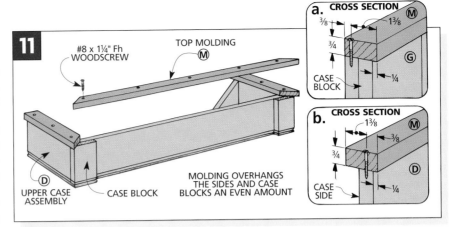

11 #8 x 1¼" Fh WOODSCREW — TOP MOLDING Ⓜ — UPPER CASE ASSEMBLY Ⓓ — CASE BLOCK — MOLDING OVERHANGS THE SIDES AND CASE BLOCKS AN EVEN AMOUNT

a. CROSS SECTION Ⓜ / Ⓖ — 3/8 — 1³/8 — 3/4 — CASE BLOCK — 1/4

b. CROSS SECTION Ⓜ / Ⓓ — 1³/8 — 3/8 — 3/4 — CASE SIDE — 1/4

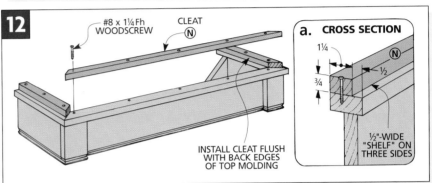

12 #8 x 1¼ Fh WOODSCREW — CLEAT Ⓝ — INSTALL CLEAT FLUSH WITH BACK EDGES OF TOP MOLDING

a. CROSS SECTION Ⓝ — 1¼ — 1/2 — 3/4 — 1/2"-WIDE "SHELF" ON THREE SIDES

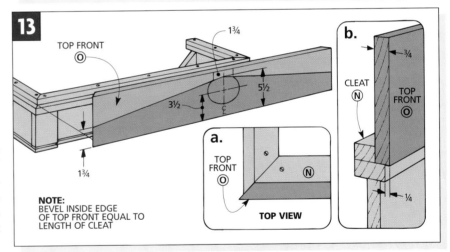

13 TOP FRONT Ⓞ — 1³/4 — 5½ — 3½ — 1³/4

a. TOP FRONT Ⓞ / Ⓝ — **TOP VIEW**

b. CLEAT Ⓝ — TOP FRONT Ⓞ — 3/4 — 1/4

NOTE: BEVEL INSIDE EDGE OF TOP FRONT EQUAL TO LENGTH OF CLEAT

Drawing An Oval

You don't have to be a whiz kid in geometry to draw an oval.

First, only four points need to be drawn. Then all you have to do is draw two circles and two arcs with a compass.

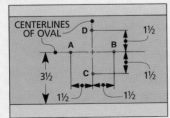

CENTERLINES OF OVAL — 1½ — 1½ — 3½ — 1½ — 1½ — A B C D

1. From the center of the oval, measure and mark the centerpoints **A**, **B**, **C**, and **D**.

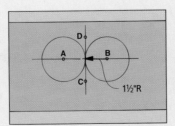

1½"R

2. Use centerpoints **A** and **B** to draw two 3" circles to form the ends of the oval.

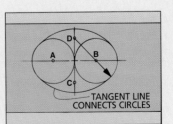

TANGENT LINE CONNECTS CIRCLES

3. Use centerpoints **C** and **D** to draw arcs connecting the tangents of the circles.

TOP SIDES. Once the top front was installed, I started work on the top sides (P); see Fig. 14. The goal here is to make the sides flush with the tapered edge on the front piece; see Fig. 14a.

The simplest way to do that is by starting with a board that's wider than needed (in my case, 3"). Then rip a 10° bevel along one edge; see Fig. 14a.

Next, miter one end to match the miter on the top front and cut the sides to length.

Then sneak up on the final width by making several rip cuts on the edge *opposite* the 10° bevel. After the top edges are flush, glue them to the cleats.

COVE MOLDING. The final piece of molding added to the top assembly is the cove molding (Q). It's attached to the top front and sides; see Fig. 15.

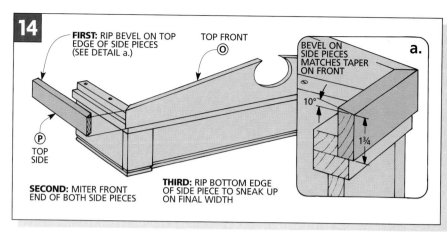

I started by cutting the molding to its finished width (1³⁄₈"). And then routing a ¹⁄₂" cove; see Fig. 15a.

Next, I cut pieces to fit on the sides and front (with overhang over the oval; see Fig. 15b). Then glue and screw these pieces in place. Note: The back edge of the cove molding is installed flush with the inside face of the top front and sides; see Fig. 16.

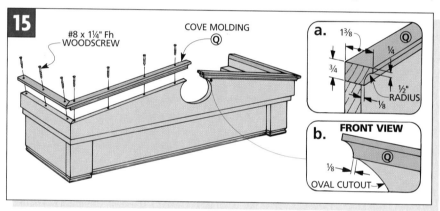

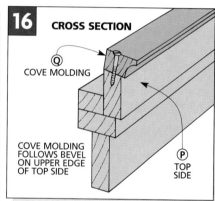

Alternate Top

By changing one component of the bookcase the whole appearance of the bookcase can change. For a simpler approach we designed a top assembly that uses straight pieces.

Actually, this is easier to construct than the other version. There aren't any tapers or bevels to cut on the top front or side pieces.

The cove molding is the same and it's glued and screwed down on top of the top front and side pieces.

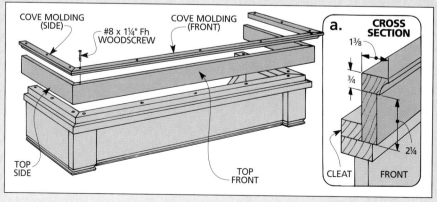

SIDE ASSEMBLIES

Once the top and bottom assemblies were complete I started work on the side assemblies. What makes them unique is they're built with double wall construction. And the space between the walls is for knockdown hardware. This hardware connects the sides with the top and bottom assemblies. A fluted cap on the front hides the hardware.

FLUTED CAP. I began to work on the side assemblies by making the fluted caps (R). They have evenly spaced flutes on the face and half flutes on each edge. To help space the flutes evenly, I used a fluting jig (see page 77).

I used an oversized blank to make each cap; see Fig. 17. They were longer than needed so stop blocks could be clamped on the ends. These blocks stop the jig in the same spot to keep the flute lengths equal.

The blanks were also wider than needed (3³⁄₄"). That way the two outside flutes could be ripped in half when cutting the blanks to their finished width; see Fig. 17a.

Now use the fluting jig, router, and a ³⁄₈"-dia. core box bit (sometimes called a round nose bit) to rout the five flutes in each cap.

Shop Tip: I made a scraper from an old hacksaw blade to clean up some burn marks on the ends of the flutes. Just file a hacksaw blade to a profile that matches the flutes. (For another tip on scraping flutes, see page 9.)

After the flutes are cut, the caps can be cut to finished size; see Fig. 17.

Next, I cut two grooves on the back side of each cap; see Fig. 17a. These grooves will accept tongues on the front edge of the side panels. When the case is ready to be assembled they help keep the cap aligned with the sides.

SIDES. After cutting the grooves in the cap, I started work on the sides. Both sides have an interior panel (S) and exterior panel (T) made from plywood; see Fig. 18. These panels are identical in length, but the interior panel is cut ¹⁄₄" narrower. This allows for the thickness of the plywood back that's installed later.

After the panels were cut to finished length and width, I rabbeted the front edge of each panel to form a tongue. The tongues are cut so they'll fit snug in the grooves on the back of the caps.

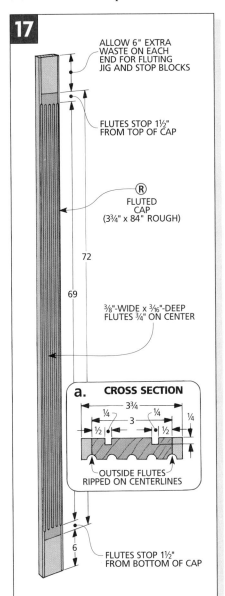

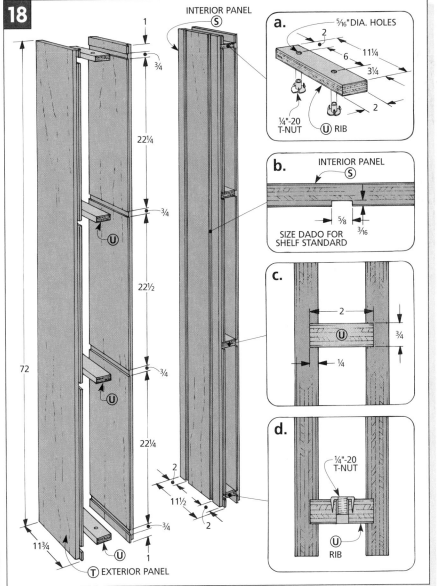

Next, four dadoes are cut on the inside walls of both the interior and exterior panels; see Fig. 18c. Plywood ribs fit in these dadoes to help keep the panels aligned.

Then two full-length grooves are cut in the inside face on both interior panels; see Fig. 18b. These are for metal shelf standards which are added later.

RIBS. After the grooves are cut, I made four ribs (U) for each side assembly; see Fig. 18a. These ribs fit in the dadoes cut in the interior and exterior panels. Two of the ribs are drilled to accept T-nuts. Bolts inserted through the top and bottom assemblies and into the T-nuts are used to draw everything together during final assembly.

SIDE ASSEMBLY. After the T-nuts are installed in the ribs, the side units can be assembled. First glue and install the ribs in the dadoes; see Fig. 18. As you install them, remember to put the ribs with the T-nuts at the top and bottom locations.

Then glue and clamp the fluted caps on the front of both side assemblies.

ALIGNMENT BLOCKS. To help put the bookcase back together if it's taken apart, alignment blocks (V) are added to the upper and lower case assemblies. They automatically align the sides and the cases.

First, the blocks are cut to fit into the top and bottom openings in the sides; see Fig. 19. Chamfer the edges so it's easy for the sides to slip over the blocks.

Next, glue and screw the blocks to the top and bottom panels; see Figs. 20 and 20a.

Then drill oversize holes through the blocks and top and bottom panels. The larger holes make it easier to get the bolts aligned with the T-nuts.

INSTALLATION. After the holes were drilled, I attached the sides to the upper and lower case with bolts and washers; see Fig. 21.

BACK. Now measure the opening for the back (W) and cut it to size; see Fig. 22. (Note: The back butts up against the *inside* edge of both exterior panels.) Finally, screw the back in place with No. 8 x 1¼" flathead woodscrews.

SHELVES

To support the shelves, I used metal shelf standards that are readily available at most home and building centers and hardware stores. They're installed

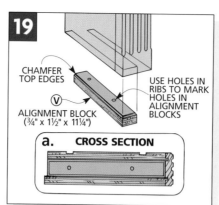

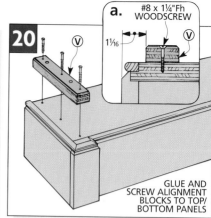

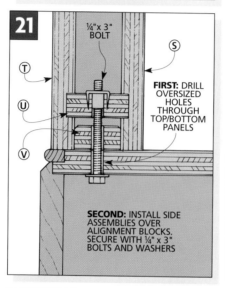

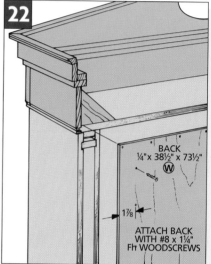

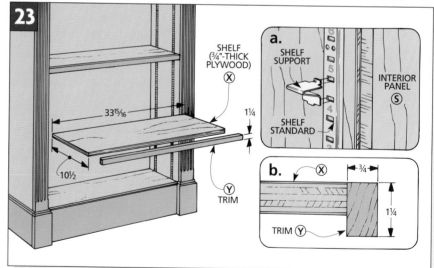

in the grooves you cut earlier in the interior panels.

One thing to keep in mind as you install the standards is to check that they're positioned in the same direction (the numbers stamped on the brackets are all right side up); see Fig. 23a. Then use the nails that came with the standards to hold them in place.

SHELVES. The last step is to make the shelves (X); see Fig. 23. They're cut to fit between the standards.

To strengthen the shelves and hide the edges of the plywood, I added trim pieces (Y) to the front of each shelf; see Fig. 23b. Glue and clamp the trim pieces in place so they're flush with the top of the shelves. ∎

When I first saw the shop drawings for the classic bookcase, I was pleased. Nice design, basic joinery, and useful, too. Then I saw the flutes (vertical grooves running up and down the caps). These would be interesting.

My first question was how to make them. Right away I knew it would be with a core box bit in the router. But what's the best way to rout the flutes an equal distance apart? What was needed was some sort of indexing jig.

The jig in the photo is the result. It has just two main parts. A piece of hardboard that replaces the base plate on the router; see Fig. 1. And a set of spacer strips attached to the hardboard.

SPACER STRIPS. The spacer strips are the key to the jig. The width of each spacer is critical — it should equal the desired distance between the centers of the flutes; see Fig. 1b.

The two outside strips act as fences for guiding the jig on the workpiece; see Fig. 1a.

BASE PLATE. The base plate should be cut long enough to accommodate the strips on either side of the bit plus the width of the workpiece; see Fig. 2.

Then cut two slots parallel to the long edge of the plate. These are for securing the strips; see Fig. 1.

SET-UP. To set up the jig, start by positioning the spacer strips in relation to the bit; see first drawing in Fig. 2.

Then the clamping strip needs to be positioned so it rides along the other edge of the workpiece; see second drawing in Fig. 2.

Now the router bit can be adjusted to the desired depth of the flutes. And the flutes routed; see "Using the Jig" below.

Shop Note: It's a good idea to start with a test piece to get a feel for using the jig. And it helps if the test piece is the same width as the actual workpiece.

STOPPED FLUTES. For stopped flutes, like on the bookcase, simply clamp a block on each end of the workpiece; see Fig. 3.

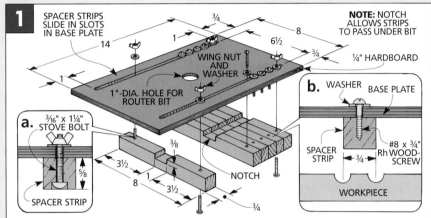

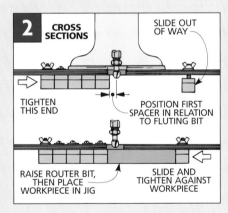

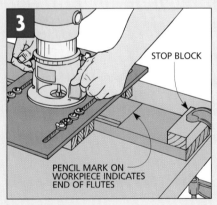

Using the Jig

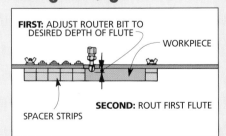

1 *Position the outside strip so there will be a shoulder left along the edge of the workpiece. Then rout the first flute with a 3/8" core box bit.*

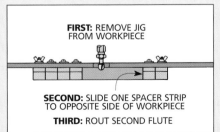

2 *Remove the jig and loosen the next spacer strip. Then move it to the opposite side of the workpiece, retighten, and rout the next flute.*

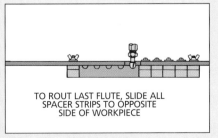

3 *Continue moving the spacer strips and routing until all the flutes are complete. Then cut the workpiece to finished width and length.*

CRAFTSMAN BOOKCASE

This bookcase was designed to be built like the original — with a combination of machinery and handwork.

This bookcase is a good example of Craftsman-style furniture. Sturdy mortise and through tenon construction, square pegs, and shop-made door pulls. The design is simple and straightforward.

When Gustav Stickley started designing furniture like this in the early 1900's, he had the "common man" in mind. Out with the ornate — furniture should be simple and functional. The result was the Craftsman style. (Sometimes it's called "Mission" style furniture.)

MACHINE AND HAND TOOLS. But Stickley was not just concerned with design. Furniture also had to be well-built in the tradition of the master craftsman. And his furniture was built with a combination of machinery and handwork.

I think that's what I like most about this bookcase. It's built in the same tradition. The heavy and repetitive tasks (the cutting, planing, and drilling) can be done by machine. The finer details (the through tenons, square pegs, and door dividers) require some careful handwork. And the whole process reflects Stickley's concern for quality and craftsmanship.

WOOD. You might be surprised to see that I used cherry to build the bookcase. Much of the Craftsman-style furniture was originally built out of quartersawn oak. But after doing a little research I discovered that cherry was used by Stickley as well.

Once it darkened to a deep brownish-red, I thought the cherry would look better with the brass ball-tipped hinges I wanted to use.

FINISH. To protect the bookcase, I brushed on four coats of General Finishes Royal Finish (Satin). While this finish isn't an authentic Craftsman finish, I did follow Stickley's technique in one way. I waxed the bookcase after

the finish had set a few days (to give it time to fully cure).

I applied several coats of a high quality paste wax. The one I found was a mixture of carnauba and beeswax.

To apply the wax, wipe on a thin layer with a cotton cloth and let it dry for a few minutes. (Several thin coats are easier to apply than one thick one.) Then buff it to a shine with a clean cloth.

EXPLODED VIEW

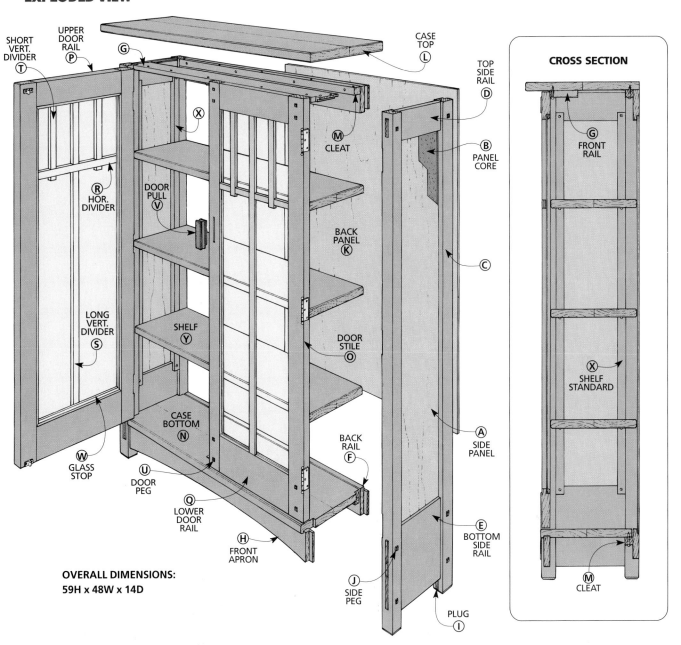

SHORT VERT. DIVIDER (T)

UPPER DOOR RAIL (P)

(G)

CASE TOP (L)

CROSS SECTION

TOP SIDE RAIL (D)

CLEAT (M)

(X)

HOR. DIVIDER (R)

DOOR PULL (V)

LONG VERT. DIVIDER (S)

SHELF (Y)

CASE BOTTOM (N)

BACK PANEL (K)

(B) **PANEL CORE**

(C)

DOOR STILE (O)

GLASS STOP (W)

DOOR PEG (U)

LOWER DOOR RAIL (Q)

BACK RAIL (F)

(A) **SIDE PANEL**

(E) **BOTTOM SIDE RAIL**

FRONT APRON (H)

SIDE PEG (J)

PLUG (I)

OVERALL DIMENSIONS:
59H x 48W x 14D

CROSS SECTION

(G) **FRONT RAIL**

(X) **SHELF STANDARD**

(M) **CLEAT**

MATERIALS LIST

WOOD

A	Side Panels (4)	¼ ply - 9³/₁₆ x 44³/₁₆
B	Panel Cores (2)	⅛ hbd x 9³/₁₆ x 44³/₁₆
C	Posts (4)	1¾ x 1¾ - 58
D	Top Side Rails (2)	1 x 3½ - 11⅝
E	Btm. Side Rails (2)	1 x 9½ - 11⅝
F	Back Rails (2)	¾ x 3½ - 41½
G	Front Rail (1)	¾ x 3½ - 42¼
H	Front Apron (1)	¾ x 3¾ - 41½
I	Plugs - Posts (4)	⅜ x ½ - 2⁵/₁₆
J	Pegs - Sides (12)	⅜ x ⅜ - 1⁵/₁₆
K	Back Panel (1)	¼ ply - 41½ x 49½
L	Case Top (1)	1 x 14 - 48

M	Cleats (2)	1 x 1 - 40½
N	Case Bottom (1)	1 x 11¼ - 41¼
O	Door Stiles (4)	1 x 2¹⁷/₃₂ - 51⅞
P	Upr. Door Rails (2)	1 x 3½ - 19⅛
Q	Lwr. Door Rails (2)	1 x 5 - 19⅛
R	Horiz. Dividers (2)	½ x 1 - 15⅞
S	Long Ver. Divid. (2)	½ x 1 - 44⅛
T	Shrt. Ver. Divid. (4)	½ x 1 x 11⁵/₁₆
U	Pegs - Doors (16)	⅜ x ⅜ - ¹³/₁₆
V	Door Pulls (2)	¾ x 1⅛ - 4
W	Glass Stops (1)	⅜ x ⅜ - 20 ft. rough
X	Shelf Stand. (4)	⅝ x 1 - 45½
Y	Shelves (3)	1 x 10⅝ - 40⁷/₁₆

HARDWARE SUPPLIES

(12) No. 6 x 1" Fh woodscrews
(23) No. 8 x 1½" Rh woodscrews
(8) No. 6 x ⅝" Fh woodscrews
(3 pair) 2½" x 2" Ball-tipped hinges
(4) Double-ball door catches
(12) Shelf pins
(100) ⅝" Wire brads
(2) 15¾ x 44" Glass panes*

*Note: I used ⅛"-thick tempered glass. Have the glass cut to fit the opening on the back of each door, minus ⅛" in both length and width, so it will fit easily.

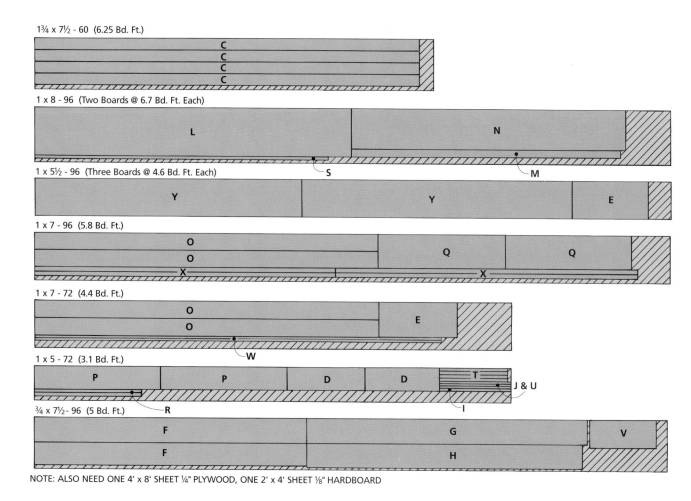

1¾ x 7½ - 60 (6.25 Bd. Ft.)

1 x 8 - 96 (Two Boards @ 6.7 Bd. Ft. Each)

1 x 5½ - 96 (Three Boards @ 4.6 Bd. Ft. Each)

1 x 7 - 96 (5.8 Bd. Ft.)

1 x 7 - 72 (4.4 Bd. Ft.)

1 x 5 - 72 (3.1 Bd. Ft.)

¾ x 7½ - 96 (5 Bd. Ft.)

NOTE: ALSO NEED ONE 4' x 8' SHEET ¼" PLYWOOD, ONE 2' x 4' SHEET ⅛" HARDBOARD

PANELS

To build this Craftsman bookcase, I started by making the framed side units. When making a framed panel, I generally use plywood for the panel. Unlike solid wood, plywood isn't drastically affected by changes in humidity.

I designed each side unit to have ½"-thick plywood panels with two good sides. (Both the inside as well as the outside of each panel can be seen.) But finding ½" cherry plywood with two good faces isn't easy. And it's quite expensive.

Instead, I cut two pieces of ¼" cherry plywood to make each panel; see Fig. 1. Then these side panels (A) can be set back-to-back so there are two good sides. Note: All the plywood pieces for this project can be cut from one 4x8 sheet of ¼" plywood.

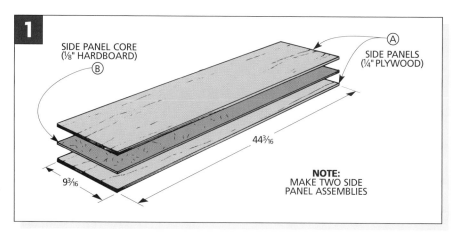

NOTE:
MAKE TWO SIDE PANEL ASSEMBLIES

But there's still a problem. Most ¼" hardwood plywood is quite a bit less than ¼" thick. The plywood I used was actually only a hair over ³⁄₁₆" thick. So to get the panels closer to ½" thick (they don't need to be exact), I sandwiched a ⅛"-thick piece of hardboard between the panels to serve as a panel core (B); see Fig. 1.

One other point. The three layers for each panel could be glued together. But you don't have to. The frames built around the panels will hold them together just fine.

SIDE UNITS

Now, a grooved frame can be built around each side panel.

First, I cut all the pieces for both side frames; see Fig. 2. The posts (C) are cut from 1³⁄₄"-thick stock. The top (D) and bottom side rails (E) from 1" stock.

GROOVES. The grooves in the posts and rails must match the thickness of the panel. And the grooves should be centered on each piece.

Since the posts and rails are different thicknesses, each requires its own setup to cut the grooves. Here, you have two options. Either reset the fence. Or keep the fence in the same position, but clamp a shim to it; refer to Fig. 5.

To find the thickness of the shim, figure the difference between the thickness of the posts and rails (³⁄₄" in my case). Then, divide this number by two. My shim ended up ³⁄₈" thick; see Fig. 5.

SET UP. To cut the grooves, I first mounted a ³⁄₈" dado blade in the table saw and raised it ³⁄₈"; see Fig. 3. Then I set the fence so the blade was slightly off-center on the piece.

I cut the groove in two passes, flipping the board between each pass; see Figs. 3 and 4. (This centers the groove.) Note: Test the setup with a scrap piece.

Once the groove is cut, check if the panel fits. If you need to, adjust the fence and make another test cut.

CUT GROOVES. When the test piece fits, cut the grooves on the four posts.

Next, to cut the grooves in the top and bottom rails, either reset the fence or add the shim; see Fig. 5.

Easier Frame and Panel Assembly

When making framed panels, grooves are usually cut in the frame to fit the panel. But that doesn't mean it will go together easily.

If the panel or frame is twisted or bowed, it can be difficult getting them together.

To make it easier to assemble and avoid tearout on the edges of the grooves, I first round over the edges of the panel with a sanding block.

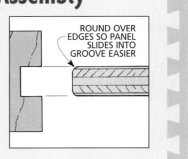

ROUND OVER EDGES SO PANEL SLIDES INTO GROOVE EASIER

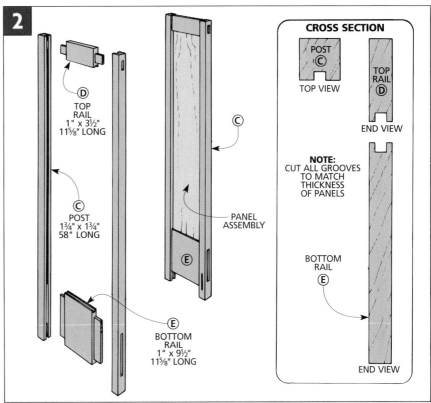

2

TOP RAIL
1" x 3½"
11⅝" LONG

POST
1¾" x 1¾"
58" LONG

BOTTOM RAIL
1" x 9½"
11⅝" LONG

PANEL ASSEMBLY

CROSS SECTION

POST (C)
TOP VIEW

TOP RAIL (D)
END VIEW

NOTE: CUT ALL GROOVES TO MATCH THICKNESS OF PANELS

BOTTOM RAIL (E)

END VIEW

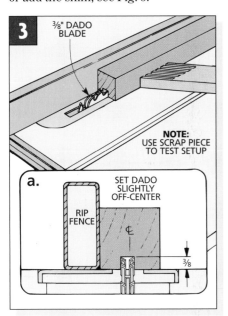

3

³⁄₈" DADO BLADE

NOTE: USE SCRAP PIECE TO TEST SETUP

a. SET DADO SLIGHTLY OFF-CENTER

RIP FENCE

₵

³⁄₈

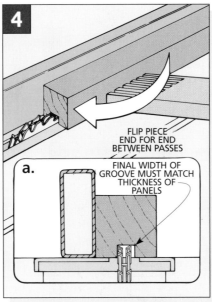

4

FLIP PIECE END FOR END BETWEEN PASSES

a. FINAL WIDTH OF GROOVE MUST MATCH THICKNESS OF PANELS

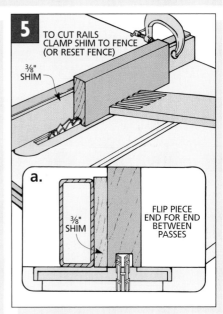

5

TO CUT RAILS CLAMP SHIM TO FENCE (OR RESET FENCE)

³⁄₈" SHIM

a. ³⁄₈" SHIM

FLIP PIECE END FOR END BETWEEN PASSES

TENONS

Like a lot of Craftsman-style furniture, this bookcase has mortises and through tenons. These demand careful handwork, but you actually get to see the joints. (For more on this joint; see page 90.)

I usually start with the mortises. But this time, I worked backwards. The tenons are cut first to fit the grooves (already cut in the posts). Like a mortise, the grooves act as a gauge for sizing the tenons.

TWO TENONS. There are two different length tenons on each of the rails; see Fig. 6. On the front end is a long tenon that fits all the way through the front posts. But the tenon in back is shorter. It stops short in a typical (blind) mortise.

TWO STEPS. The setup for both the top and bottom rails is the same; see Figs. 7 and 8. Each tenon is cut in two steps. First, cut the cheek of the tenon; see Step 1. Note: Use a scrap piece and test the thickness of the tenons with the grooves in the posts.

Next, set the piece on edge and cut the tenon to width; see Step 2.

MORTISES

After all the tenons are cut on the rails, it's time to cut the mortises in the posts. Again, there are two types of mortises: through and blind.

All the mortises are the same width as the grooves for the panels. This makes the setup easy. Just position the post so a $1/2$"-dia. drill bit is centered in the groove. Then clamp a fence to the drill press table so it's against the post.

BLIND MORTISES. After laying out each mortise, I drilled the blind ones in the back posts first; see Fig. 9. (Drill them $1^5/16$" deep. This allows $1/16$" for excess glue.)

THROUGH MORTISES. When the mortises in the back posts are complete, drill the mortises through the front posts. Shop Note: To prevent chipout on the faces of the posts and inside the grooves, drill these mortises halfway through from both sides.

MORTISES FOR APRON. There's one more set of mortises to cut in the front posts only. An apron joins the two front posts at the bottom. It requires a $1/4$"-wide by $9/16$"-deep mortise on the *inside* edge of both front posts; see Fig. 9.

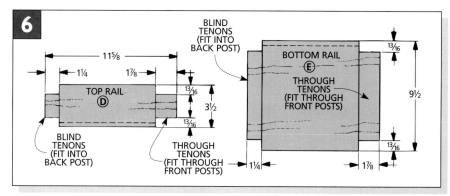

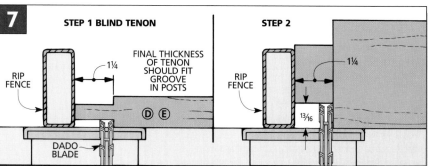

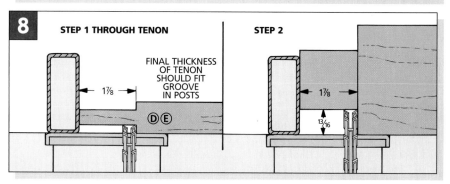

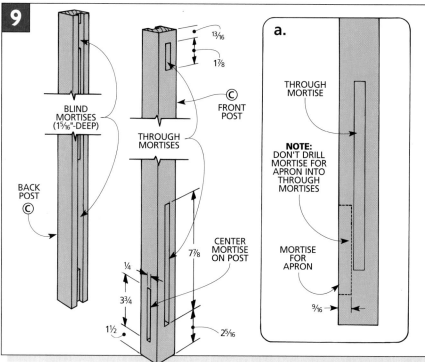

RAILS & APRON

Before the side units can be put together, there must be some way to connect them. So next I cut out the pieces that connect the units.

CUT TO SIZE. Begin by cutting two back rails (F) and a front rail (G) to size; see Fig. 10. Then cut out a front apron (H). (Note: The width of this apron should match the mortises in the posts — the apron doesn't have a top or bottom shoulder; refer to Fig. 15a.)

RABBETS. To hold these pieces, I rabbeted some of the side unit pieces. Each top side rail (D) is rabbeted on the top inside edge to hold the front rail; see Figs. 10b and 11.

Then the two back posts (C) are rabbeted on the back inside edges to hold the back rail and the back panel (added later); see Figs. 10a and 12.

The back rails (F) also hold the back panel in place. So, I rabbeted the back edges of these rails too; see Fig. 13.

Shop Note: All these pieces don't end up identical — they're actually mirrored. So mark the pieces before you cut the rabbets.

TONGUES. The next step is to cut tongues on the pieces that will connect the side units; see Fig. 10. Rabbet the ends of the back rails (F) and the front rail (G); see Figs. 13 and 14. The tongues should fit the rabbets in the side pieces.

After these rabbets are cut, the front rail needs to be notched at the front cor-

ners to fit around the front posts; see Figs. 10b and 14. When in place, the rail should set back 1" from the front. This allows the rail to act as a door stop.

RABBET APRON. The last piece to rabbet is the front apron (H); see Fig.

15. Again, you're creating tongues on the ends. But this time, they fit the mortises in the posts.

The apron also has a gentle arc on the bottom that can be laid out and cut at this time; see Fig. 15a.

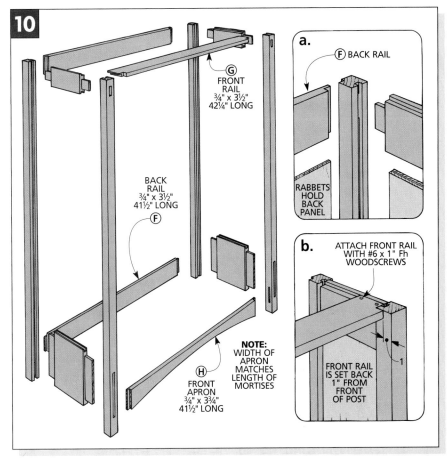

10

a. (F) BACK RAIL

RABBETS HOLD BACK PANEL

b. ATTACH FRONT RAIL WITH #6 x 1" Fh WOODSCREWS

FRONT RAIL IS SET BACK 1" FROM FRONT OF POST

(G) FRONT RAIL 3/4" x 3 1/2" 42 1/4" LONG

BACK RAIL 3/4" x 3 1/2" 41 1/2" LONG (F)

NOTE: WIDTH OF APRON MATCHES LENGTH OF MORTISES

(H) FRONT APRON 3/4" x 3 3/4" 41 1/2" LONG

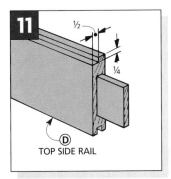

11 1/2 1/4

(D) TOP SIDE RAIL

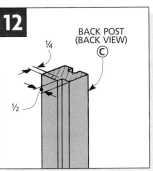

12 BACK POST (BACK VIEW) (C) 1/4 1/2

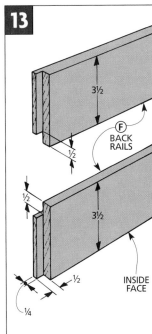

13 3 1/2 (F) BACK RAILS 1/2 1/2 3 1/2 1/2 INSIDE FACE 1/4 1/2

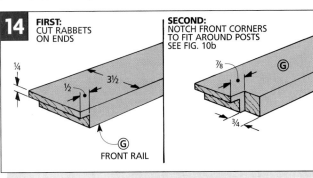

14 FIRST: CUT RABBETS ON ENDS   SECOND: NOTCH FRONT CORNERS TO FIT AROUND POSTS SEE FIG. 10b

1/4 1/2 3 1/2 (G) FRONT RAIL   7/8 (G) 3/4

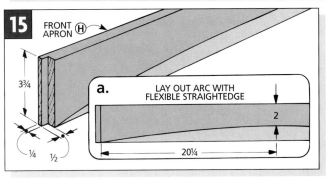

15 FRONT APRON (H) 3 3/4 1/4 1/2

a. LAY OUT ARC WITH FLEXIBLE STRAIGHTEDGE 2 20 1/4

CASE ASSEMBLY

The bookcase is almost ready to be assembled. But first, I added some small details.

The first step is to fill the grooves at the bottom of the posts; see Fig. 16. (The top of the posts will be covered by the case top later.) To do this, I cut a plug (I) to fit each groove. Note: Make sure you don't cover the mortises already cut in the posts.

CHAMFERS. The next step is to rout a $1/8$" chamfer on the *bottoms* of all the posts; see Fig. 17. This has two benefits. It gives the posts a finished look, and it also helps minimize chipout if the case should ever be dragged across the floor.

Another thing I did was to sand chamfers on the ends of *all* the tenons. This "dresses up" the through tenons, giving them a finished look. And on the tenons that fit the blind mortises, the chamfer allows room for excess glue.

SANDING BLOCK. There are a number of ways to chamfer the tenons, but I made a simple sanding block that chamfers both edges at the same time; see Fig. 18.

To make the block, I cut a groove in a piece of scrap with the dado blade set $3/8$" deep. The width should equal the thickness of the tenon minus $1/8$". (This will create a $1/16$" chamfer on both sides

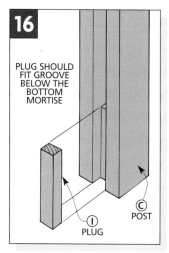

16 PLUG SHOULD FIT GROOVE BELOW THE BOTTOM MORTISE

© POST
① PLUG

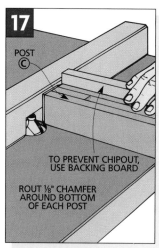

17 POST ©

TO PREVENT CHIPOUT, USE BACKING BOARD

ROUT $1/8$" CHAMFER AROUND BOTTOM OF EACH POST

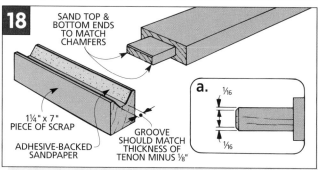

18 SAND TOP & BOTTOM ENDS TO MATCH CHAMFERS

$1\frac{1}{4}$" x 7" PIECE OF SCRAP

ADHESIVE-BACKED SANDPAPER

GROOVE SHOULD MATCH THICKNESS OF TENON MINUS $1/8$"

a. $1/16$ $1/16$

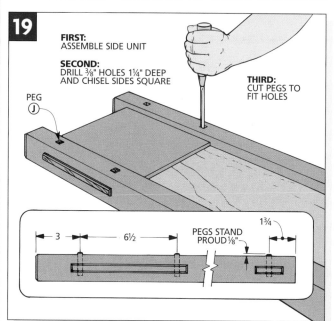

19 FIRST: ASSEMBLE SIDE UNIT

SECOND: DRILL $3/8$" HOLES $1\frac{1}{4}$" DEEP AND CHISEL SIDES SQUARE

THIRD: CUT PEGS TO FIT HOLES

PEG ①

3 $6\frac{1}{2}$ PEGS STAND PROUD $1/8$" $1\frac{3}{4}$

Scraping And Sanding Corners

Normally I like using a hand scraper and sanding block for scraping and sanding. But on a frame and panel, it can be hard to get right down into a corner with a scraper or typical sanding block.

Instead, I use two tools shaped for the job.

To scrape out a corner, I use a razor blade from a utility knife; see Fig. 1. It works great for scraping away glue smudges and when I need to cut away dried beads of glue.

To use the razor blade,

hold it at an angle and push or pull it with the grain of the wood — just like a hand scraper. And, always push or pull the

blade in the direction it's angled. (This way it won't cut into the workpiece.)

To sand a corner, I make a sanding block with

beveled ends and beveled sides; see Fig. 2. The pointed ends allow me to get the sandpaper right up against the corner.

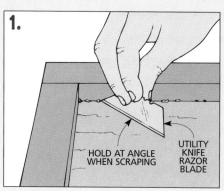

1. HOLD AT ANGLE WHEN SCRAPING

UTILITY KNIFE RAZOR BLADE

2. BEVELED EDGES ALLOW SANDING BLOCK TO GET INTO CORNER

Adding Decorative Pegs

It used to be that a long tenon needed to be pinned in a mortise. But these days, with improved wood glues, a peg doesn't have to do anything but look good. Careful work is the key to good looks.

It helps to think of a peg in a hole as a tenon in a mortise. So the procedure is similar to cutting a mortise and tenon joint.

Lay out the mortise on the outside face of the stile; see Fig. 1. Then drill inside the marks to a consistent depth.

Next, use a small chisel to square up the corners of the mortise; see Fig. 2.

To make the pegs, cut a long strip to size so it's about $1/32$" thicker than the width of the mortise. (You want it to be a tight fit.) Then cut the pegs from the strip; see Fig. 3.

Now, sand the buried end of each peg to a slight taper. And sand a very slight decorative chamfer around the top end of each peg.

The square pegs look best if they stick out $1/8$" beyond the face of the frame. To set the pegs consistently with a ruler would be difficult. So to set the pegs accurately, I made a depth stop from a scrap of $3/4$"-thick hardwood; see Fig. 4. Then I drilled a hole in the depth stop the same

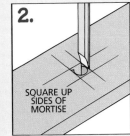

1. LAY OUT MORTISES ON GOOD FACE OF LEG

DRILL HOLE INSIDE LAYOUT MARKS

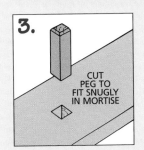

2. SQUARE UP SIDES OF MORTISE

3. CUT PEG TO FIT SNUGLY IN MORTISE

4. DRILL $1/8$"-DEEP HOLE

DEPTH STOP

a. DEPTH STOP SETS PEGS TO SAME HEIGHT

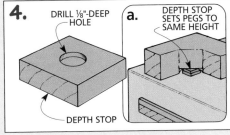

depth as I wanted to set the pegs ($1/8$" proud).

To glue in a peg, brush some glue down into the mortise with a small artist's brush and start to tap the peg into place. Now set the stop block over the peg and tap the block lightly with a hammer until it bottoms out against the frame.

---

of the tenon; see Fig. 18a.) Next, I tilted the blade 45° and beveled both sides of the groove.

To use the sanding block, stick adhesive-backed sandpaper on the beveled edges or use standard sandpaper and rubber cement. Then sand the tenons. Check them often to make sure the chamfers are consistent. After the tenon "bottoms out" on the block, sand the top and bottom ends to match, using a regular sanding block.

ASSEMBLE THE SIDE UNITS. To assemble the case, I began by gluing up the side units; see Fig. 19.

PIN TENONS. After both side units are assembled, their tenons can be pinned; see Fig. 19a and the tip box above. First, drill and square up the holes. Next, cut pegs (J) to fit them. Then glue the pegs in place so they stand $1/8$" proud.

ASSEMBLE THE CASE. To connect the two side units, glue the front apron (H) between them and dry assemble all the other rails; see Fig. 20. After the front apron dries, remove each of the rails and drill shank holes and pilot holes. Then glue and screw them back in place; refer to Figs. 10b and 20a.

BACK PANEL. After the case is assembled, I cut a back panel (K) from $1/4$" cherry plywood to fit in the rabbets

in the back of the case; see Fig. 20. But don't nail the panel in yet. It's easier to work on the inside if it's not in place.

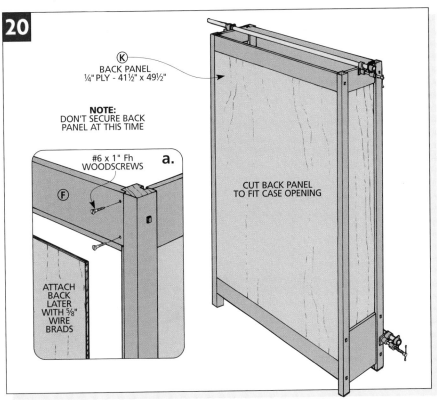

20

(K) BACK PANEL
$1/4$" PLY - $41 1/2$" x $49 1/2$"

NOTE:
DON'T SECURE BACK PANEL AT THIS TIME

#6 x 1" Fh WOODSCREWS

(F)

a.

CUT BACK PANEL TO FIT CASE OPENING

ATTACH BACK LATER WITH $5/8$" WIRE BRADS

CASE TOP

The next step is to add the case top and bottom. Begin by gluing up enough 1"-thick stock to make both panels; see Figs. 21 and 24. Now, cut the case top (L) 4" longer and 2" wider than the case; see Fig. 21. Then rout chamfers on the top and bottom edges (except the back); see Fig. 21a.

In the front, the case top is screwed directly to the front rail, refer to Fig. 23a. In the back it's secured with a cleat.

CLEAT. First, cut the cleat (M) to fit between the back posts; see Fig. 22. (Make two — you'll use one for the bottom shelf later.) Then drill two sets of shank holes in the top cleat; see Fig. 22a. One set will be used to attach the cleat flush with the top edge of the back rail. The other will secure the top.

A 14"-wide top will expand and contract quite a bit with seasonal changes in humidity. So rather than fight it, I decided to allow the panel some freedom to move by drilling oversize shank holes in the *front* rail. This way, the case top stays flush with the back of the case, but it can still expand toward the front without splitting.

BOTTOM

The bottom of the case involves a bit more work than the top. Begin by cutting the case bottom (N) to fit between the side panels (A); see Figs. 24 and 25.

NOTCHES. To fit in the case, each corner must be notched; see Fig. 25. The notches at the front corners are $1/8$" *wider* ($1^7/8$") than the posts; see Fig. 24.

The notches at the back are only 1" wide; see Fig. 24. This creates a tiny gap so the bottom can expand toward the back; refer to Fig. 25a.

Shop Note: To get a clean cut, I first scored the notches with an X-Acto knife. Then I used the miter gauge with an auxiliary fence and cut them with the panel standing on edge.

GROOVE. The next step is to cut a groove on the case bottom to fit over the front apron; see Figs. 24a. Then, rout a chamfer around the front edge.

CLEAT. Just like the case top, the bottom also requires a cleat (M); see Figs. 22 and 25. But there are two differences. First, the cleat isn't flush with the back rail. It's 1" *down* from the top.

Also, the shank holes should be oversize to allow for movement; see Fig. 25a.

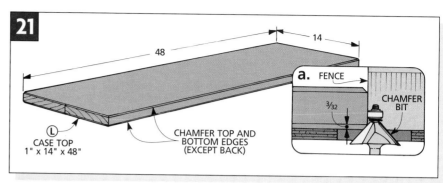

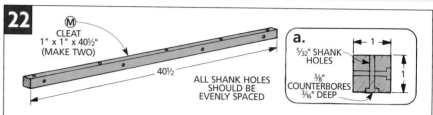

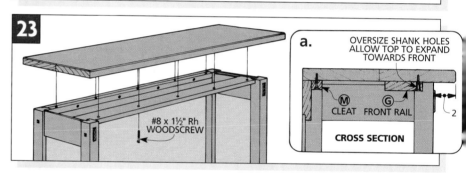

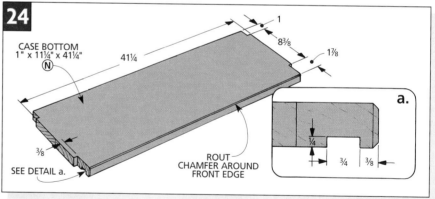

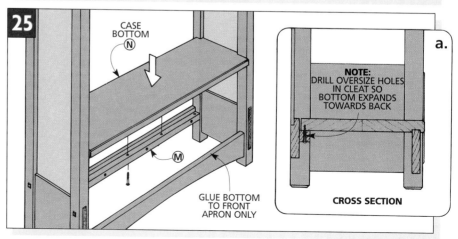

DOORS

You might want to add the shelves next. But to position the top shelf so it hides behind the dividers in the doors, it makes sense to build the doors first.

FRAMES. To begin, cut 1"-thick door stiles (O) and the upper (P) and lower door rails (Q) to fit the case opening; see Fig. 26. Note: The final size of both doors should allow a 1/16" gap between the case and the doors on all four sides.

The door frames are joined together with mortise and tenons; see Fig. 26.

After each frame is assembled, rabbet the back for the glass; see Fig. 27. Then chisel the corners square.

DOOR DIVIDERS. All the dividers in the doors are more for appearance than anything else. That's because the glass for each door is installed in one large piece — not individual panes.

To make the door dividers, first cut the 1/2"-thick horizontal dividers (R) and long vertical dividers (S) to fit between the rabbets in the frames; see Figs. 28 and 29. Then cut the short vertical dividers (T).

HALF LAPS. The dividers are joined to the door frame and to each other with half laps; see Figs. 28a and b. So first, I rabbeted the ends of all the pieces. Note: Just rabbet one end of the short vertical dividers.

Next, I cut half laps in the horizontal dividers; see Fig. 28b. Then I cut the mating half laps in the vertical pieces (on the face opposite the rabbet).

DIVIDER ASSEMBLY. Now, glue the dividers together. Then set the assembly in the rabbets in the door frame and mark the location of each divider; see Fig. 29.

To get the assembly flush with the *front* of the door, you'll need to cut mortises in the rabbets; see Fig. 29a. Once they fit, glue them in place.

PEGS. To complete the doors, pin each tenon with two door pegs (U); see Fig. 26. These are shorter than the other pegs, but still stand proud 1/8".

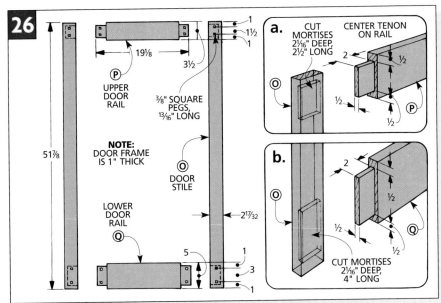

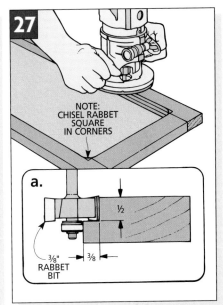

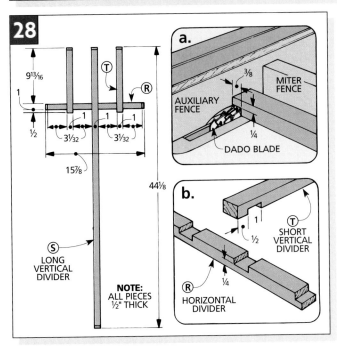

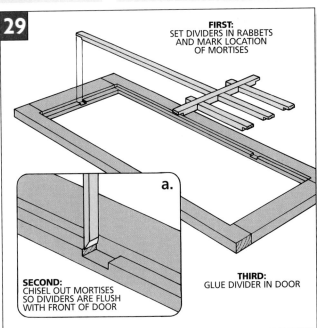

INSTALLING THE DOORS

At this point, the doors should fit with a $^1/_{16}$" gap between the case and each door. The doors still need to be trimmed though — I didn't allow for any gap between them yet. I found it easier to mount the doors first. Then come back later and remove and trim them to create the center gap.

MOUNT HINGES. The ball-tipped hinges I used created a $^1/_{16}$" gap when mortised and mounted flush with the posts and the doors.

To mount the hinges, first lay out their locations on the posts and the doors; see Fig. 30. Then cut out most of the waste with a router. And clean up the shoulders with a chisel.

After drilling pilot holes, install the hinges and mount the doors in place; see Fig. 30b.

TRIM DOORS. Now the center stiles of each door can be trimmed. To do this, determine how much needs to be trimmed to create a $^1/_{16}$" gap. Then to keep the doors identical, I removed them and planed the same amount off each door. (I used a hand plane, but a jointer will also work.)

ADD CATCHES. Next, reattach the doors and mount the catches to hold them closed. Since any door can have a tendency to twist, I installed double-ball catches at both the top and bottom of each door; see Figs. 30a and 30c.

REMOVE DOORS. To add the door pulls and the glass, I found it easiest to remove the doors once again. But first, I marked the position of the horizontal dividers on the inside faces of the corner posts; see Fig. 30. (Later, these marks will show you where to position the top shelf.)

ADD DOOR PULLS. At this point I added the door pulls. To do this, first I cut a mortise in the front of each door to accept a pull; see Fig. 31a. Then I made my own door pulls (V) (refer to the box on the opposite page) and glued them into the mortises.

GLASS STOPS. All that's left to add to the doors is the glass. Of course you don't want to add the glass until after the case has been finished, but now is a good time to cut the glass stops (W).

The finished dimensions of the glass stops are $^3/_8$" x $^3/_8$", and they have a chamfer cut along one corner, see Fig. 32a. (The chamfer provides a flat face to nail $^5/_8$"-long wire brads into.)

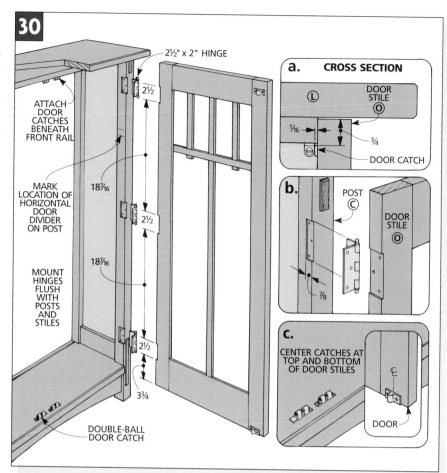

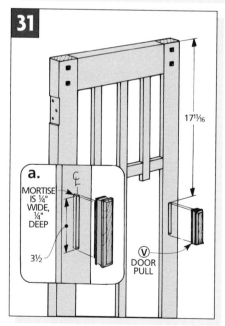

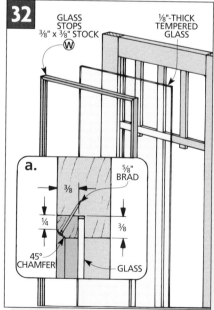

The safest way to make these glass stops is to start with an extra-wide (1$^1/_2$") blank and rout the chamfer first. Then come back and rip the pieces to final width ($^3/_8$") off the waste side of the blade.

The glass stops are mitered at the corners; see Fig. 32. It's tougher to remove mitered stops later, but they look better than butt joints. To determine the correct lengths, I find it's easiest to measure for each one individually and then creep up on the final cut until they just fit.

STANDARDS & SHELVES

You're almost done — the shelves are all that are left. They rest on spoon-style shelf pins that fit into shelf standards.

SHELF STANDARDS. To make the standards, start by cutting four $5/8$"-thick shelf standards (X) to fit between the top and bottom side rails; see Fig. 33. Note: Add 2" for the rabbets that will be cut on the ends.

Now, cut a 1"-long rabbet on both ends of each standard; see Fig. 33a. Set the standards in place and mark the position of the top shelf; see Fig. 34. (It should line up behind the horizontal door dividers.)

SHELF PIN HOLES. Before attaching the standards to the sides, drill the holes for the shelf pins; see Fig. 33. (You can drill additional holes if you want. This will allow you to adjust the position of the shelves later.)

SHELVES. For the shelves (Y), glue up three 1"-thick shelf blanks and cut them to length so they fit loosely between the corner posts ($1/16$" less); see Fig. 34. To determine the width of the shelves, measure from the rabbet

for the back panel to the back of the door. Then subtract $1/8$". (In my case, this came out to be $10^5/8$". The important thing is that the shelves aren't tight against the back of the door.)

Finally, chamfer the top and bottom

edges of the shelves and set each of them in place.

BACK PANEL. The last step on the bookcase before finishing is to install the back panel. To do this, I used $5/8$" wire brads. ∎

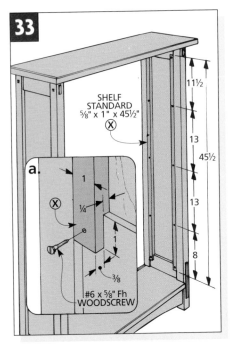

33

SHELF STANDARD
$5/8$" x 1" x $45^1/2$"
Ⓧ

$11^1/2$
13
$45^1/2$
13
8

a.

1
$1/4$
Ⓧ
1
$3/8$
#6 x $5/8$" Fh
WOODSCREW

34

ROUT $3/32$"
CHAMFERS

$40^7/16$ $10^5/8$

SHELF
Ⓨ

CUT SHELVES
TO FIT BETWEEN
POSTS

Shop-Built Door Pulls

Stickley's furniture company made all of its own hardware. While I didn't make my own hinges or door catches, I did make the wooden door pulls.

The pulls are cut from an extra-long blank of $3/4$"-thick cherry, see Fig. 1. The extra length makes the blank safer to work with.

The first step to shaping the pulls is to rout a chamfer around each end of the blank; see Fig. 2.

Next, rout a cove around each end using a $1/2$"-dia. core box bit; see Fig. 3.

Now, before cutting the pulls from the blank, form tenons to fit the mortises in the doors; see Fig. 31a on

the opposite page.

Since the tenon is in the middle of the blank and not at the end, this cut looks a little odd. Just cut or rout dadoes around the blank; see Fig. 4.

All that's left now is to sand the pulls smooth and

cut them from the blank. Then glue them into the mortises in the doors.

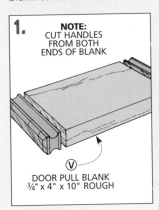

1. NOTE:
CUT HANDLES
FROM BOTH
ENDS OF BLANK

Ⓥ
DOOR PULL BLANK
$3/4$" x 4" x 10" ROUGH

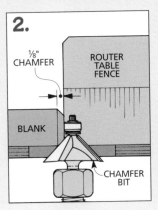

2. $1/8$"
CHAMFER
ROUTER
TABLE
FENCE

BLANK

CHAMFER
BIT

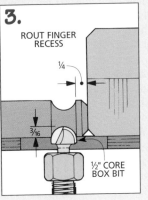

3. ROUT FINGER
RECESS
$1/4$

$3/16$

$1/2$" CORE
BOX BIT

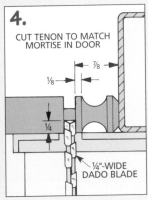

4. CUT TENON TO MATCH
MORTISE IN DOOR

$7/8$
$1/8$
$1/4$

$1/4$"-WIDE
DADO BLADE

One of the strongest joints you'll find on a project is a mortise and tenon. And a *through* mortise and tenon joint not only gives you a strong joint, but a decorative one as well.

When the tenon is glued into the mortise, the two fit together like the handle in the head of a hammer; see photo. The end grain on the tenon is a decorative contrast to the long grain on the sides of the mortise.

PERFECT FIT. The main reason for gluing a long tenon into an open mortise is usually appearance. And for the *best* appearance, the parts of the joint have to be cut perfectly.

If there are any gaps where the tenon comes out of the mortise, it will be apparent — but it probably won't be the look you were expecting. That's why I follow a special sequence when cutting a through mortise and tenon joint.

SEQUENCE. Does that mean a through mortise and tenon joint is made differently than a traditional blind mortise and tenon? Not exactly. The mortise is usually cut first, then the tenon is cut to fit the mortise. So far, no difference. But because the fit of the joint is so important, I take a couple extra steps as is explained on the following pages.

Note: Sometimes there's a good reason to reverse the sequence and cut the *tenon* first. (The Craftsman bookcase is an example; refer to page 82.) But the actual cutting operation is the same.

OPTIONS. Like an ordinary mortise and tenon joint, a through mortise and tenon joint has some options. For one, the leg is often thicker than the rail; see photo above and the drawing at right.

But this is mostly a design decision — the parts could just as well be the same thickness.

And how far beyond the leg should the tenon stick out? It could be flush to the outside of the leg (right in photo) or stand a little proud with chamfered edges (left in photo). Again, it's mostly a design decision.

Finally, a through mortise and tenon joint is often pinned with small wood pegs through the cheeks of the tenon (left in photo). In the past this was done to lock the tenon in the mortise to create a stronger joint. But with the improved glues available today, the pegs are mostly for appearance. (See page 85 for more on installing pegs.)

HOW THE JOINT WORKS

There's more to a through mortise and tenon joint than one piece of wood sticking through another. If the parts fit together properly, the joint is strong in several directions. And it looks good, too.

The load-bearing strength of the joint comes from the bottom edge of the tenon resting in the bottom of the mortise; see drawing. It's what supports a panel in a frame or a top on a table.

The shoulders around the tenon give the joint resistance to racking and twisting — and hide imperfections.

Probably the strongest part of a through mortise and tenon joint is the fit between the cheeks of the tenon and the cheeks of the mortise. When properly glued, the bond between the cheeks of the two pieces will produce a joint that's practically unbreakable.

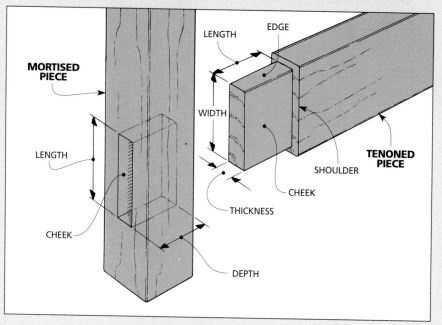

Cutting the Mortise

The key to cutting a perfect through mortise is uniformity. The tenon opening should have very straight edges to fit tight around the tenon.

Here are a couple tips — and a guide — to make cutting a perfect mortise easier.

LAY OUT ENDS. I start by laying out (marking) the mortise on the *outside* face of the workpiece; see Step 1. To do this, first use a try square and a sharp pencil to draw a line indicating the top and bottom edges of the mortise. Then use a square to extend these lines around to the opposite (inside) face.

MARK SIDES. Next, I mark the sides of the mortise. And for the most accuracy on the sides, I don't use a pencil. Instead, I make the marks using a chisel, a mallet and a shop-made guide

block; see Step 1. (Again, make the marks on the face of the workpiece where the end of the tenon will show.)

The guide block I use is simply a squared-up wood block with a shallow rabbet cut along one edge. As simple as it is, the block is surprisingly helpful.

The block helps to mark a perfectly straight line for the sides of the mortise. And after the mortise has been roughed out with a drill bit, it helps hold a chisel straight up for cleaning up the mortise.

SETTING OUT. There's a trick I use to help ensure crisp, clean edges on a through mortise. The trick is called "setting out."

To set out a mortise, first chop straight down on the chisel holding the back of the chisel tight to the guide block; see Step 1.

After marking the perimeter of the mortise, remove the guide block and make a second angled chisel cut that intersects with the first; see Step 2.

Then remove all the little three-sided

slivers from the edges of the mortise.

Now you should be able to see the outline of a perfect through mortise. All that's left is to clean out the waste.

BORE HOLES. At this point the mortise could be chopped out by hand. But it saves a lot of time (especially for deep mortises) to rough out most of the waste using the drill press; see Step 3.

To rough out the mortise, I use a Forstner bit *smaller* than the width of the mortise and drill a series of overlapping holes between the score marks.

Shop Note: For the cleanest mortise, bore halfway from each side; see Step 4.

CHISEL CLEAN. The overlapping holes will leave a series of "ripples" in the mortise. To remove these ripples and also complete the mortise — I use a chisel and the guide block to pare the sides of the mortise; see Step 5. (Again, work from both sides.)

Finally, to insert the tenon more easily, I "back cut" the mortise slightly; see Step 5a.

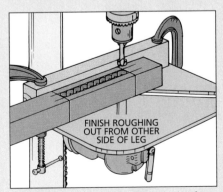

1 First mark ends of the mortise using a try square and pencil. Then make a block for marking the sides with a chisel.

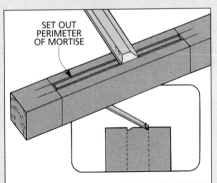

2 After scoring sides with a chisel, "set out" the mortise by chiseling a slight bevel inside score lines. Set out ends too.

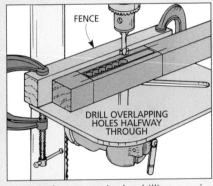

3 Rough out mortise by drilling a series of holes inside the score lines. Use a Forstner bit smaller than the mortise.

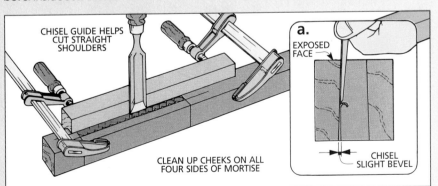

4 Finish roughing out the mortise from the opposite side of workpiece. But keep the same face against the fence.

5 Complete the mortise by chiseling the sides of the mortise smooth and flat. Use the guide block to keep the chisel straight up and down. After cutting from both sides of the mortise, chisel a slight bevel from the good face.

Cutting the Tenon

A tenon can come in any shape or size. But there's only one thing that counts — how well it fits in a mortise.

One of the easiest ways to cut a tenon is to use a dado blade in the table saw. And to help set up the saw just right, I start by cutting a tenon on a test piece. (Use a piece of wood that's the same thickness and width as the actual workpiece.)

TEST THICKNESS. To begin work on the tenon, raise the dado blade and make a shallow cut across one end; see Step 1. Then flip the piece and make a second pass on the opposite face.

Shop Note: For the most control — and the cleanest cut — I cut tenons using the miter gauge with an auxiliary fence attached. This helps prevent chipout as the blade exits the workpiece.

Now check the test tenon in one of the completed mortises; see Step 2. The idea is to sneak up on the height of the blade until the end of this short tenon fits the mortise perfectly — not too tight and not too loose.

CUT CHEEKS. When the thickness of the tenon is set, the tenon can be cut to length; see Step 3. To do this, I again use the miter gauge and auxiliary fence. But this time the rip fence on the table saw is used as a stop.

Position the rip fence so the distance between the outside of the dado blade and the fence equals the desired length of the tenon. Now, cut the tenon by making several passes over the dado blade for each cheek.

CUT SHOULDERS. The last thing to do is cut the tenon to the desired width. You may have to change the height of the dado blade to determine this width. (Note: Again, I test the height first by making cuts near the end of a test piece of the same width.)

To keep the position of the shoulder consistent all the way around the workpiece, I use the same fence setup as I did when cutting the cheeks. The only difference is that the workpiece is stood on edge now as it passes over the blade; see Step 4.

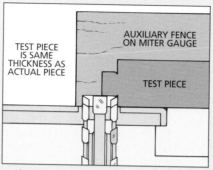

1 Begin cutting the tenon on a test piece. Sneak up on thickness of tenon by adjusting height of the dado blade.

2 Test the fit of the tenon in a mortise. If the tenon is too tight, raise the height of the dado blade and cut again.

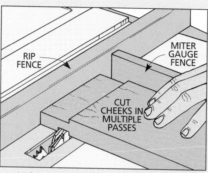

3 When the blade is adjusted for the correct thickness, cut the tenon to the desired length. Use the fence as a stop.

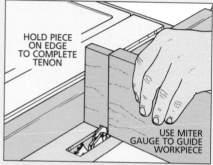

4 Now the tenon can be cut to width. Don't move the fence, but the height of dado blade may need to be adjusted.

Design Notes

When you start designing a bookcase, one of the first questions is whether the shelves will be strong enough to hold a full set of books — without sagging.

Books are heavy — heavier than they look. A set of encyclopedias, for example, weighs in at about 100 lbs. When you're dealing with that much weight, the shelves in a bookcase have to be designed to hold up. The materials you use for the shelves and any method of reinforcing the shelves become important, or the shelves will sag.

Shelf Materials

There are three materials commonly used for shelves: particleboard, plywood, and solid wood. Each has advantages and disadvantages, and each sags differently.

PARTICLEBOARD. For most situations the worst material for shelves is particleboard. The wood fibers in particleboard run every which way. This helps keep particleboard from expanding and contracting, but does little to prevent sag.

However, particleboard may be the best choice in two cases. First, if cost is a factor, particleboard is very inexpensive. That's why most knock-down shelves you see at discount stores are particleboard (complete with fake wood grain). A second reason to use particleboard is that it's a good flat base for veneer.

One key thing with particleboard is that there's a number of different kinds available. Some sag more than others. For example, low density, class 1, particleboard has a minimum average "E" factor of only .15. (The "E" factor refers to the "modulus of elasticity" or stiffness of the board. The higher the "E" factor, the less the board will sag.) Medium density, class 1, particleboard has an "E" factor of .25. And high density, class 1, particleboard has an "E" factor of .35. (That compares to 1.24 for Eastern white pine, one of the weakest pines.)

If you decide to use particleboard for shelving, high density particleboard (sometimes called "cabinetmaker's grade" rather than "underlayment") would be the best choice since it's stiffer (but also considerably heavier).

PLYWOOD. What about making shelves out of plywood? Plywood doesn't usually warp like solid wood and it's dimensionally stable. These characteristics are important in a bookshelf where you want flat shelves that won't expand and contract with changes in humidity. But plywood sags more than solid wood.

In solid wood the individual wood fibers run along the length of a board. These fibers resist stretching (sagging) along their length so a board of solid wood is stiffer along its length than its width. Plywood is constructed so that *some* of the fibers (every other layer) run along the length. This keeps a plywood shelf dimensionally stable but the shelf won't be as stiff as one of solid wood.

Another factor contributing to the weakness in plywood is that it's usually built up of different species of wood. The face plies may be a strong hardwood such as oak, but the inside plies could be anything, even basswood. And there might be voids that weaken it further.

CREEP. There's something else I should mention about plywood and particleboard. When you first load books on a bookshelf, the shelf may sag slightly. But over a period of time there's an additional sag called "creep."

Particleboard and plywood are especially susceptible to creep because of the glue used to bond the material together. The glue stretches over time. The particleboard shelves that you put up in the shop to hold paint cans might not sag at first, but may look like a sway-back horse after a couple years.

There's another thing about creep. In all wood materials creep increases if the temperature or humidity increases. Also green wood creeps much more than dried wood. (That's another reason to use kiln-dried lumber.)

SOLID WOOD. If your only goal in building shelves is to prevent sag, solid wood is the best choice. All the fibers in it run along the length, and as long as the shelf is put into the cabinet lengthwise, sag will be kept to a minimum.

If the wood is particularly dense, such as oak or birch, the wood cell walls are thick, there are more of them, and they tend to resist the compression and tension forces that take place within a shelf under load. So it's usually better to make shelves out of a denser wood. As an example, yellow birch has an "E" factor of 2.01, red oak 1.82, black cherry 1.49, and ponderosa pine 1.26.

Sag Testing

How much sag is too much? Your eye will start to see a deflection (sag) of about $1/32$" per running foot. For example, if a shelf is 36" long, it shouldn't sag more than $3/32$" at the center. That means a $1/16$" sag would be acceptable, but a $1/8$" sag would become very noticeable.

SOME TESTS. Before building the shelves in this book, I did some simple tests to compare the sag of different shelf materials. I tested pieces of $3/4$" high density particleboard, $3/4$" oak plywood, and 4/4 ($3/4$" actual thickness) white oak — each piece was cut 10" wide by 36" long.

To set up the tests, I supported the piece at each end and measured the distance from the bottom of the piece to the top of the bench. Next I placed six bricks (42 pounds

42 Lbs. of Bricks on 10" x 36" Shelf	Amount Of Sag
$3/4$" High Dens. Particlebd.	$7/32$"
$3/4$" Oak Plywood	$6/32$"
4/4 ($3/4$") White Oak	$2/32$" *
6/4 ($15/16$") White Oak	$1/64$" *
*Acceptable Sag $3/32$" Per 36"	

total) at the center of the shelf and measured the sag; see photo.

RESULTS. The particleboard sagged about $7/32$"; see the chart above. The oak plywood sagged a little less than $6/32$", and the solid oak only sagged $2/32$". Using the $1/32$" per foot rule (or $3/32$" over three feet), only the solid wood was acceptable.

Recommended Spans

If you're designing a cabinet, what's the greatest length (span) a shelf can be without an objectionable sag? There are three things to consider: 1) how the load is distributed, 2) the expected load, and 3) the shelf material.

LOAD DISTRIBUTION. For the tests in the box on page 93, I wanted to determine the "worst possible situation" for the distribution of the load. So I used six bricks (42 pounds), and placed them right in the center of the shelf.

However, in a normal situation the weight would be distributed over the entire shelf. This is the assumption used to develop the chart at right.

EXPECTED LOAD. Another factor used to determine maximum span is the total expected load — the longer the shelf, the more weight it has to hold.

A running foot of average-size books weighs about 20 pounds. So a three-foot shelf filled with average-size books would have to support about 60 pounds. (Encyclopedias would weigh more, and paperback books less.)

SHELF MATERIAL. The third factor is the type of material used — particleboard, plywood, or solid wood. Each has a different "E" factor, as discussed on the opposite page.

GUIDELINES. Taking all three factors into consideration, the chart at right shows some general guidelines for the maximum span for shelves to avoid an objectionable sag.

The most practical approach is to use 4/4 (3/4"-thick) stock (or plywood with reinforcement; see section below). This will produce shelves with minimum sag and the best visual appearance.

Maximum Span Recommendation for 10"-Wide Shelf Full of Books	
3/4" Particleboard	24"
3/4" Plywood	30"
4/4 (3/4") Solid Stock	36"
6/4 (1 5/16") Solid Stock	60"

Reducing Sag

Even though plywood and particleboard sag more than solid wood, there are times when they might be a better choice for shelves. That's because they aren't as likely to warp or expand and contract with changes in humidity. But when using these materials (as well as solid wood), there are some steps you can take to reduce the sag.

DISTANCE. First, determine if there's some way to design the cabinet to decrease the span of the shelf. If you reduce the span, you can reduce the sag. A rule of thumb is if you cut the span in half, the sag will be one eighth as much as the original.

For example, a shelf that's 36" long may sag 1/8" at the center. If it's supported so each half is 18" long, the sag on each half will be reduced to 1/64".

INCREASE THICKNESS. Another solution is to increase the thickness of the shelf. A thicker shelf will dramatically increase the shelf's rigidity. If you double the thickness, you can reduce the sag to one-eighth of the original.

To test this I cut a piece of 1 5/16"-thick white oak to the same dimensions as the test shelves shown on page 93. When the bricks were piled on, the deflection was only a little over 1/64", which compares to a sag of 4/64" (1/16") for 3/4" stock.

Supporting the center of a shelf, or making the shelf thicker may not be realistic solutions. A better approach to reducing sag might be to add support to the edges or under the shelf. It's common to see shelves with a face strip added to the front edge. This is not just decoration or a way to cover the edge of the plywood or particleboard. Facing strips are a functional addition to the shelf — the strips are there to add stiffness.

A shelf is like a 2x4 laid flat on its side. If you lay a 2x4 flat between two end supports and add weight, it would definitely sag. But if you tipped the same 2x4 up *on edge* and added the weight, there would be very little sag.

FACE STRIP ON EDGE. The same principle applies if you add a face strip on edge to the front of a shelf. To test how much this helps a plywood shelf, I added a 1 1/4"-wide vertical strip of 3/4" oak stock to the front of the plywood shelf and measured the sag. Without the strip the plywood sagged 6/32". But with the vertical facing strip, it sagged only 2/32"; see drawing below.

HORIZONTAL FACE STRIP. What about adding a horizontal solid face strip to the front of the plywood shelf? It covers the edge plies and doesn't decrease the shelf space. I tested this arrangement by adding a 1 1/4"-wide strip horizontally to the front of the plywood. The plywood sagged a little more than 4/32". That's an improvement over the plywood without a face strip but not as good as the strip on edge.

UNDERSHELF SUPPORT. Sometimes a vertical strip is needed for strength but doesn't fit the design of the project. One way to hide the support is to put it under the shelf. The support takes up shelf space, but it can be fit into a groove cut in the bottom of the shelf.

I tried gluing (with epoxy) a 1/16"-thick by 1"-wide reinforcing strip of aluminum into a groove routed in the bottom of the plywood. Adding this thin strip of aluminum under the shelf was comparable to adding the 3/4" wooden strip vertically to the face — sag was reduced to only 2/32".

I also decided to try adding some wood reinforcing strips under the shelf where they wouldn't show. I cut a couple pieces of 1"-wide hardwood strips (with a tongue and bullnosed face) and glued them into grooves cut into the bottom of the plywood shelf. It sagged about 3/32", and I'd consider that acceptable on a three foot long shelf. That's the design I used for the oak bookcase shown on page 60.

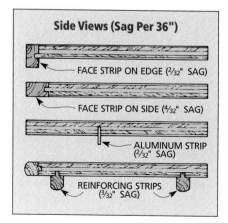

Side Views (Sag Per 36")

FACE STRIP ON EDGE (2/32" SAG)

FACE STRIP ON SIDE (4/32" SAG)

ALUMINUM STRIP (2/32" SAG)

REINFORCING STRIPS (3/32" SAG)

Sources

One of the first things we take into consideration when designing projects at *Woodsmith* is the hardware. Does it complement the project and is it appropriate? Is it affordable? And, most important, is it commonly available?

We *don't* design projects that require hard-to-find hardware. You'll probably be able to find most of the hardware and finishing supplies for the projects in this book at your local hardware store or home center. Sometimes, though, you may have to order the hardware through the mail. If that's the case, we've tried to find reputable national mail order sources with toll-free phone numbers (see box at right).

In addition, *Woodsmith Project Supplies* also offers hardware kits for some of the projects listed in this book (see box below).

NOTE: We *strongly* recommend that you get all of your hardware and supplies in hand *before* you begin building any project. From time-to-time hardware manufacturers go out of business and they change dimensions and styles. There's nothing more discouraging than completing a project and then finding out that the hardware is no longer available or the size or design has changed slightly.

Woodsmith Project Supplies

At the time of printing, the following project supply kits were available from *Woodsmith Project Supplies*. These kits include hardware, but you must supply any lumber, plywood, or finish. For current prices and availability, call toll free:

1-800-444-7527

Quilt Rack
(pages 7-11) ....No. 790–100

Country Shelf
(pages 16-20) ....No. 786–100

Craftsman Bookcase
(pages 78-89) ....No. 790–200

Mail Order Sources

Some of the most important "tools" I have in my shop are the mail order catalogs kept on the shelf. They're filled with special hardware, tools, finishes, lumber, and supplies that I can't always find at my local hardware store or home center.

I've found that these catalogs have excellent customer service and are only a free phone call away. You should be able to find all the supplies for the projects in this book in one or more of these catalogs.

One more thing. It's amazing what you can learn about woodworking just by looking through these free catalogs. If you don't have the following catalogs in your shop, I strongly recommend that you call and have each one sent to you. (And, of course, you'll be put on their never-ending mailing lists.)

Woodcraft
210 Wood Co. Industrial Park
P.O. Box 1686
Parkersburg, WV 26102-1686
800–225–1153

A must! Has just about everything (tools, hardware, finishing, wood) for the woodworker.

The Woodworkers' Store
4365 Willow Drive
Medina, MN 55340
800–279–4441

Probably the best all-around source for general and specialty hardware, but also has tools, finishes, lumber, and veneer.

Woodworker's Supply
1108 N. Glenn Road
Casper, WY 82601
800–645–9292

Excellent source for power tools and accessories, hardware, and finishing supplies.

Trendlines
135 American Legion Highway
Revere, MA 02151
800–767–9999

Another complete source for power tools and accessories. Some hardware and supplies.

Cherry Tree Toys
P.O. Box 369
Belmont, OH 43718
800–848–4363

The best source for wooden parts (spindles, legs, turnings, craft items, etc.). Also includes finishing supplies and some hardware.

WoodsmithShop Catalog
P.O. Box 842
Des Moines, IA 50304-9661
800–444–7002

Our own source for practical jigs, useful tool accessories, *Woodsmith* project supplies, finishes, lumber, and kits.

Garrett Wade
161 Ave. of the Americas
New York, NY 10013
800–221–2942

The "Bible" for hand tools but also one of the best sources for finishing supplies and high quality power tools. This catalog is filled with useful information and tips so much of it reads more like a good woodworking book than a typical mail order catalog.

Constantines
2050 Eastchester Road
Bronx, NY 10461
800–223–8087

One of the original woodworking mail order catalogs. Known for veneers and inlays but also has a good collection of hardware and finishing supplies.

Craftsman Wood Service Co.
1735 West Cortland Court
Addison, IL 60101
800–543–9367

This catalog has been in existence for over 65 years. They carry a wide variety of veneers and domestic and foreign lumber. Also finishing supplies, wooden parts, hardware, small tools, plans and books.

If You Enjoyed This Book,
You're Going To Love Our Magazines

Woodworking and Home Improvement:

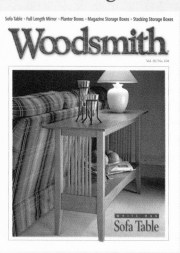

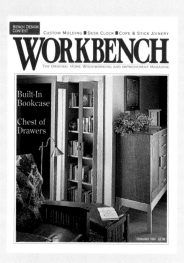

▲ *Woodsmith*, America's most popular fully-illustrated project magazine, continues to deliver detailed project plans, useful techniques, and easy-to-follow instructions to those who love woodworking. Published bi-monthly.

▲ *ShopNotes*, filled with practical tips and jigs, step-by-step woodworking techniques, shop projects and unbiased tool reviews, will help you get the most out of your shop, while saving you time and money! Published bi-monthly.

▲ *Workbench* contains creative furniture, shop, and woodworking home improvement projects, like kitchen cabinets, storage ideas, built-ins, decks, and more, all with detailed illustrations and photos. Published bi-monthly.

Gardening:

Cooking:

◄ Packed with practical, step-by-step gardening information, and hands-on tips and techniques about garden design and color, *Garden Gate* will help you create the beautiful garden you have always wanted. Published bi-monthly.

► Loaded with step-by-step photographs plus tips to help make your cooking easier and more eye-catching. *Cuisine* is the ideal bi-monthly magazine for those who love cooking and want to bring some variety to their dinner table.

To bring any of these exciting magazines to your home, or for more information,
Call Toll Free: 1-800-333-5075